THE
DOG
ATE IT

THE DOG ATE IT

Cooking for Yourself and Your Four-Legged Friends

Linda West Eckhardt
and Barbara Bradley
with Judy Kern

GOTHAM
BOOKS

GOTHAM BOOKS
Published by Penguin Group (USA) Inc.
375 Hudson Street, New York, New York 10014, U.S.A.
Penguin Group (Canada), 90 Eglinton Avenue East, Suite 700, Toronto, Ontario M4P 2Y3, Canada (a division of Pearson
Penguin Canada Inc.); Penguin Books Ltd, 80 Strand, London WC2R 0RL, England; Penguin Ireland, 25 St Stephen's Green,
Dublin 2, Ireland (a division of Penguin Books Ltd); Penguin Group (Australia), 250 Camberwell Road, Camberwell, Victoria
3124, Australia (a division of Pearson Australia Group Pty Ltd); Penguin Books India Pvt Ltd, 11 Community Centre,
Panchsheel Park, New Delhi – 110 017, India; Penguin Group (NZ), cnr Airborne and Rosedale Roads, Albany, Auckland
1310, New Zealand (a division of Pearson New Zealand Ltd); Penguin Books (South Africa) (Pty) Ltd, 24 Sturdee Avenue,
Rosebank, Johannesburg 2196, South Africa

Penguin Books Ltd, Registered Offices: 80 Strand, London WC2R 0RL, England

Published by Gotham Books, a member of Penguin Group (USA) Inc.

First printing, October 2006
10 9 8 7 6 5 4 3 2

Copyright © 2006 by Linda West Eckhardt and Barbara Bradley
All rights reserved

Gotham Books and the skyscraper logo are trademarks of Penguin Group (USA) Inc.

Library of Congress Cataloging-in-Publication Data
Eckhardt, Linda West, 1939–
The dog ate it : cooking for yourself and your four-legged friends / Linda West Eckhardt and
Barbara Bradley with Judy Kern.
p. cm.
Includes index.
ISBN 1-592-40229-1 (trade pbk.)
1. Dogs—Food—recipes. I. Bradley, Barbara. II. Kern, Judy. III. Title.
SF427.4.E25 2006
636.7'085—dc22   2006000811

Printed in the United States of America
Set in Guardi with Jimbo
Designed by Sabrina Bowers

Without limiting the rights under copyright reserved above, no part of this publication may be reproduced, stored in, or in-
troduced into a retrieval system, or transmitted, in any form, or by any means (electronic, mechanical, photocopying, record-
ing, or otherwise), without the prior written permission of both the copyright owner and the above publisher of this book.

The scanning, uploading, and distribution of this book via the Internet or via any other means without the permission of the
publisher is illegal and punishable by law. Please purchase only authorized electronic editions, and do not participate in or
encourage electronic piracy of copyrighted materials. Your support of the author's rights is appreciated.

While the author has made every effort to provide accurate telephone numbers and Internet addresses at the time of publication, neither the publisher nor the author assumes any responsibility for errors, or for changes that occur after publication. Further, the publisher does not have any control over and does not assume any responsibility for author or third-party
Web sites or their content.

Dedicated to:

RUBY,

AFTEN,

JILLI,

DOOLEY,

DICKIE,

MAXINE,

AND GRACIE

The dogs who have inspired us

Contents

Acknowledgments

Thanks to our agent, Susan Ginsburg, who continues to guide us well; our editor, Erin Moore, daughter and granddaughter of veterinarians who believed in the project from the beginning; our typists, Dianne and Trish Miller; the veterinarians who advised us, Dr. Rao Mallampati and Dr. Bonnie Gray; our national focus group, who gave us paws up or paws down on the recipes; the Arizona pugs Maurice and Beauregard; the New Mexico dogs Bosco and Aggie; Miss Shih Tzu New Jersey, Evie; the Californians, Teddy, Mae-Mae, and Snuffy; and last but not least, Sheri Woolston, who endured yapping dogs at her feet for almost a year while we wrote the book.

INTRODUCTION

The Dog Ate It

"I wouldn't feed that to my dog!" How many times have we heard or said that when confronted with a particularly unappealing or inedible meal? And where did such an idea come from anyway? Aren't our dogs our best friends, our children, members of our family? More than half the dog owners who responded to a recent survey conducted by the American Pet Association indicated that they were more attached to their dogs than to any particular human. So why would we even dream of feeding our dog something we wouldn't eat ourselves?

We know what you're thinking—it's easier. And in a way we're sure that's true, but isn't most commercial pet food just fast food for dogs? Well, we're sure you've heard about what happened to that guy who ate nothing but McDonald's for breakfast, lunch, and dinner for a month. Would you want to do that to your dog? Okay, you say, but nobody's going to cook specially for his or her dog. Maybe not, but you undoubtedly cook for yourself, so what if you could both eat the same thing? That's what this book is all about—cooking for two (or the whole family, for that matter).

Although our dogs are certainly central to our lives, we are both extremely busy, and yet we've had no problem preparing and feeding them—and ourselves—the recipes in this book. In fact, since we have to eat anyway, it's a relief not to have to worry about whether we've run out of canned food or kibble for our canine companions.

We just know that whatever we're eating, they'll be happy to join us. Dogs really want to eat "people food" anyway, so why not oblige them with recipes you know are healthy and good for you both?

When we cook for our dogs and ourselves, we try to start with the best raw ingredients we can lay hands on. Barbara is an ardent shopper of organic produce and meats. Linda raises a large organic garden. Both of us try to avoid additives in the diet—be it ours or theirs—so cooking for the dogs becomes a natural extension of what we are doing for ourselves.

Neither of us is a veterinarian, nor do we have degrees in nutrition, but we've owned dogs since we were children, and this is the food we feed our own dogs every day. Linda's, at the time of this writing, are Ruby, an eighteen-month-old Gordon setter, and Aften, a fifteen-year-old Muensterlander. Barbara's are Dicky and Dooley, fourteen-year-old twin bichon frises. Their mother, Jilly, recently passed on at the age of seventeen. Our group also extends to occasional dinner parties with Evie, a three-year-old shih tzu, and some long distance taste-testing by a pair of four-year-old pugs named Maurice and Beauregard. All of them, we are delighted to say, are healthy, lean, and energetic.

Dogs were domesticated (or maybe they domesticated us) more than 14,000 years ago, and for most of that time, there was no commercial dog food. We don't honestly know what they ate back in ancient Egypt, but in more modern "olden" days, before Purina produced the first commercial dog food about sixty years ago—and many moons before Eukanuba or Science Diet—the family dog ate table scraps.

Many of the ailments that plague dogs today—including obesity, diabetes, kidney problems, and skin disorders—can be linked to the invention of commercial pet food, and can be cured with a balanced diet comprised of human-grade meat, whole grains, and fresh vegetables. Fleas, dental problems, and bad breath rarely trouble dogs who eat properly. Given a proper diet and a reasonable exercise regimen, our companion animals can live to a healthy and vigorous old age.

I doubt there are many dog owners who can honestly say they've never fed their pets from the table. So why not get back to basics and, at the same time, provide your "best friend" and yourself with healthy, nutritious, and delicious meals like Chow Bella Burger Bites, Lamb Shish Kebabs, and Veal Breast with Veggies?

In the pages that follow, you'll find recipes for these dishes as well as hors d'oeuvres, salads, desserts, and breakfast or brunch dishes you and your dog can share on those lazy weekend mornings when you settle down with the paper and he settles down with a toy. There will also be treats for the two of you to share, along with party ideas.

And because there are some foods we wrinkle our noses at that nevertheless set doggie noses twitching, we've also included a chapter devoted to "dogs-only" meals to have on hand for those nights when you're dining out (or ordering in Chinese).

ONE

What Dogs Need to Eat and Be Healthy

According to Juliette de Baïracli Levy, world-renowned natural dog-rearing expert and author of *The Herbal Book for the Dog: A Complete Handbook of Natural Care and Rearing,* which was originally published in 1947 and reprinted in 1961, dogs who live in the wild get plenty of exercise, eat fresh raw meat, drink clean water from streams, refrain from eating when they are ill, and do not fall prey to many of the ills that can plague modern-day pets.

Of course, the pampered pets sharing a household with one of the more than 44 million dog-owning humans in the United States don't have to hunt for their supper or go for days without eating. The modern lives of dogs have changed, as have the modern lives of humans. As our lives have become easier, however, most of us (both human and canine) have become more sedentary, and our food supply has become both more abundant and less healthy. Dogs certainly can and do survive on nothing but kibble, just as we could probably survive on a diet of bologna sandwiches, but that doesn't mean that these diets are good for either one of us.

We recommend that you feed your dogs animal protein plus carbohydrates in the form of vegetables and grains such as brown rice, pasta, or kasha. The animal protein portion of the diet should be comprised of 50 percent chicken, 40 percent muscle meats such as beef, lamb, and pork, and 10 percent organ meats including liver, kidney, and poultry giblets. We try to use vegetables and fruits that are in season and organic if we can get them. That way, we help ensure that the dogs receive the widest possible variety of nutrients. We also add yogurt and kefir for the friendly bacteria and variety they provide.

Our goal in this book is to put both you and your dog back on track for eating balanced meals made with fresh, natural ingredients that are tasty as well as nutritious. We know you all lead busy lives—as we've said, so do we—which is why we've made these one hundred recipes as quick and easy as possible.

On weekends we often cook up a simple stew with a couple of carrots, fresh poultry or red meat seasoned with herbs and spices such as parsley and garlic (no onion, please, because as healthy as onions may be for us, they are, unfortunately, poison for dogs), liquid, and a whole grain such as brown rice, and let it simmer until we're ready to serve it. Leftovers can then be divided into single-

How to Spot a Well-Fed Dog

Obesity in household pets is rising as rapidly as obesity in humans, and for the same reasons. Dogs fed nothing but corn- or rice-based kibble get way too many processed carbohydrates in their diet and really inadequate satisfaction, which means that (like their human counterparts) they keep eating and eating and eating. Net result? Fat, unhealthy dogs with compromised immune systems.

Bright eyes; a cool, moist nose; clean, white teeth; and clean, dry ears are the immediate clues that a dog has a healthy diet. The dog's coat should be shiny, soft, and clean. Pull up a piece of skin, and it should be soft and pliable with no visible layer of fat underneath.

Run your hands over the dog's rib cage. Except for on a roly-poly puppy, you should be able to feel the ribs under the pliable skin, and his body shape should be hourglass-like, with the belly tucked up under the ribs. The dog's muscles should feel firm, well developed, and defined, and his paws should be smooth and resilient. The nails should be firm, not cracked, sore, or brittle. The dog's anus should be clean and dry, and his urine should be light and yellow, never dark or clear.

serving portions and frozen so that you'll have a ready-cooked meal on hand for those days when you're too busy to breathe.

On work nights, a simple sauté or stir-fry like Teriyappi, served over brown rice from last night's Chinese takeout, may be just the thing to take the edge off both the stress of the day and the appetite you and your pooch have built up. Nothing fancy. Just good, fresh food that's ready in minutes.

There is a short list of foods, like the onions mentioned above, that should never be fed to dogs (see the complete list in Appendix A), but we haven't had any problem cooking around these foods.

Our Doggie Diet Dos and Don'ts

In addition to the forbidden foods listed in Appendix A, we also eschew white sugar, vegetable shortening, and all trans fats because they're unhealthy for dogs as well as people.

We add the following products, which we find in natural food stores and high-end grocery stores, in the Asian products aisle or where condiments are sold. The first three are dried and are available either in sheet form or as granules.

- dried seaweed (also called *nori*)
- sea kelp
- sea vegetable
- Spike (a natural all-purpose seasoning that replaces salt)

We use these in many of our recipes because they not only improve palatability but also provide trace minerals and vital nutrients.

The seaweed, sea kelp, and sea vegetable are interchangeable in recipes. Just use what you find. Don't stress yourself. Keep it simple. The Spike improves the taste of foods for dogs and people without adding chemicals or other unnatural ingredients. It is available both with and without salt. Buy what works for you.

Please note that, except for the dogs-only dishes, all portion sizes in this book are for "human servings." As a guideline for how much to serve your dog, please see the section on the following page.

As we've said, we are not veterinarians, nor do we claim any particular medical expertise. But we do know that this is what keeps our pets healthy, vigorous, long-lived, and out of the vet's office most of the time. That's our real goal.

In the writing of this book, we have encountered many questions from friends and dog-loving acquaintances. Here are the ones that we hear most frequently.

 How much should dogs eat?

The name of the game here is portion control, for dogs as it is for humans. You don't want to overfeed your pet any more than you should overfeed yourself. Puppies need to eat three times a day, but after about four months of age, two meals a day are plenty. We feed our dogs just enough so that they can lick the plate clean in 30 minutes or less. Then we pick up and wash their bowls until it's time for the next meal. Doing that teaches them to eat when they're served, so to speak, rather than grazing all day, which would be the doggie equivalent of our constantly picking out of the refrigerator and never eating a full or balanced meal.

Common sense should tell you that proper portion size depends on the size of the animal. We've found that dogs who eat healthy, nutritious food feel more satisfied with less, stop eating when they're full, and generally do not overeat. But as a general rule of thumb you will want to feed between 2 and 3 percent of your pet's ideal body weight—2 percent for less-active pets and 3 percent for those who are more active. Puppies up to 9 months old need anywhere from 5 percent to 10 percent of their body weight. For adult dogs, use the following quantities as your guideline.

- **Small dogs (up to 12 pounds):** a total of ¼ to ½ cup mixed meat protein, cooked or raw vegetables, and grain twice a day
- **Medium dogs (up to 35 pounds):** a total of 1 cup mixed meat, vegetable, and grain twice a day
- **Large dogs (more than 35 pounds):** a total of 2 cups or more mixed meat, vegetable, and grain twice a day

Why are the recipes in this book measured in people servings instead of dog servings?

Dogs come in many shapes and sizes. The shape and size of your dog—whether you have a Chihuahua or a Great Dane—will determine how much food your dog requires. We've provided guidelines above, but we must reiterate that most dogs won't overeat when fed a satisfying, natural diet.

The Well-Fed Dog Pantry

The following is not intended as an exhaustive inventory but rather as a short list of foods to keep in the cupboard, the refrigerator, or the freezer so that you can always cook up a dog- and people-friendly meal at a moment's notice.

MEAT AND POULTRY

90-percent lean ground beef
Chicken breasts
Chicken legs and thighs

VEGETABLES AND GRAINS

Barley
Carrots
Corn
Green and red bell peppers
Green beans
Pasta
Peas
White and brown rice
Whole wheat flour

DAIRY

Eggs
Lowfat plain yogurt

COOKING LIQUIDS

Chicken broth
Olive oil

CONDIMENTS

Garlic
Honey
Assorted dried herbs and spices

What if my dog needs to lose weight?

Dogs who eat nothing but commercial dog food are often over-weight. This poses the same health risks for them as it does for humans: diabetes, heart disease, exacerbated arthritis pain, a shortened life expectancy, and a diminished quality of life. A healthy diet of home-cooked food will usually remedy this problem, but here are some additional tips for lightening your dog's load.

- Canned green beans. For some reason, most dogs love these. Simply stirring a can of green beans (drained) into whatever it is that you're feeding your dog will increase the roughage and palatability of the food. Linda's old dog, Asher, who lived out most of his fifteen Muensterlander years before we began feeding our dogs a home-cooked, natural-food diet, would wag his tail and lick his chops at the very sight of the green bean can coming out of the pantry.
- Cottage cheese. Adds calcium without making the dog fat.
- More vegetables and small amounts of cooked oatmeal mixed into the food.

And, as with people, make sure he gets enough exercise—a longer walk wouldn't hurt either one of you. Add some vigorous rounds of chase or "fetch" to your daily routine. And watch those snacks.

 How do I start feeding my dog a home-cooked diet?

If your dog has been eating commercial dog food, you will find it easier than you could have imagined to make the transition. We do, however, suggest that you do it gradually. Take away one quarter of the commercial food and replace it with home-cooked food. After three or four days, begin to feed your dog half commercial food and half home-cooked. Soon, your dog will be happily lapping up completely home-cooked meals—and will be healthier for it!

But what if the food I cook makes my dog sick?

Making the transition gradually should help to prevent tummy upsets, but if you are concerned about diarrhea, here's the straight poop. Loose stools are often a way of purging and purifying the dog's digestive tract. Diarrhea doesn't necessarily equal illness. Once the dog's system is cleaned out, you will notice several significant changes. Your dog will be eating less because his food is more nutrient-dense, and, as a result, his stools will be smaller, well-formed, and firm.

Of course, if the diarrhea persists, you should see your veterinarian. Small dogs in particular, like small children, can become dehydrated very quickly.

 *If it wasn't for dogs, some people would never go for a walk.*—Anonymous

 Is it okay to feed my dog table scraps?

Well, that depends. If you eat a lot of fast food and junk food, do your dog a favor and don't share your meal. On the other hand, almost any wholesome, simple foods that you eat will also be good for your dog. Our dogs love salads, sushi, pasta, and many vegetables, including raw or lightly steamed carrots, green beans, broccoli, and cucumbers. All of these foods make excellent treats for dogs. If your dogs are small and have small mouths, be sure to shred the vegetables to make it easier for them to eat and digest.

Do you have any tips for easy ways to improve my dog's diet?

Sure we do.

- Give your dog a tablespoon of peanut butter on a spoon (a dog lollipop).
- Stir a tablespoon of yogurt per 25 pounds of weight into the dog's dinner.
- Give your dog one egg for every 25 pounds of weight twice a week.
- Feed your dog liver at least once a week. For a small dog up to 12 pounds, even a tablespoon at a time will help improve his health. For large dogs, over 35 pounds, up to 6 ounces will help improve skin conditions and yield many health benefits. See our liver treat recipes (pages 118 and 119) for an easy way to add liver to your dog's diet.

 Is there an easy way to brush my dog's teeth?

Giving your dog a raw, meaty bone at least once a week helps scrape his teeth clean. Choose beef marrowbones or knucklebones. Don't use pork or turkey bones because they can splinter. Chicken necks work well for little dogs, but you may need to grind them first. This is a quick and easy way to keep your dog from having bad breath, tartar buildup, and infection in the mouth.

 Sometimes my dog won't eat anything all day long. Should I worry about that?

Did you consider the possibility that your dog doesn't like your cooking? While human beings are at least courteous when they don't like a dish you've prepared, dogs give no such quarter. Dogs will reject food for reasons of their own. Don't try to force them to eat something they don't want, and know that in the wild, dogs fast about one day out of seven and this is perfectly normal. So don't panic if your dog goes off her feed for a day. She may know more than you about what is good for her. If, however, your dog continues to reject food the second day, you'd better call the vet.

 I was told to withhold water from my dog after 6 P.M. to prevent accidents in the house. What do you think of this?

Not much. Clean, fresh water should always be available. Dogs eating wet food will receive moisture through their food and, therefore, require less water than pets eating only dry food. Nevertheless, clean water should always be available. Too much dry kibble coupled with inadequate water in their diet can cause kidney stones in animals. In addition, small dogs can become dehydrated very quickly, and must always have a good supply of clean, fresh water.

 What if my dog doesn't eat everything in her bowl? Can't I just leave it and top it off for the next meal?

Do not refill half-empty bowls. You need to provide fresh food at every meal. This is particularly true in hot weather, when food left in bowls can turn bad or attract flies and other insects.

 The vet I go to says never to give dogs food from the table. He insists that commercial dog food is necessary to provide proper nutrition. What do you think?

Many veterinarians believe that dog food is better because it is formulated to meet dogs' nutritional needs. They also suggest that if you feed your dogs different meals every day, you'll never know whether they're refusing food because they're sick or because they just don't like the menu you've planned.

Our answers to these concerns are that, first of all, the meals in this book are all created to provide proper nutritional balance for you and your dog, and, furthermore, our research indicates that many commercial dog foods are made using ingredients and methods that can compromise rather than improve your dog's health. (See page 139 for our list of acceptable commercial pet foods.)

If you are concerned about feeding your dog a nutrient-dense diet, just remember to give equal parts meat, grain, and vegetables most days, and, if you wish, supplement his food with a good animal multivitamin.

As for your dog's refusing a meal he doesn't like—well, we suspect that you've done that, too. If your dog skips more than two meals in a row, he may not be feeling well, but there will probably be additional signs—is he lethargic? Out of sorts? Drinking too much or too little water? If you're an alert and observant dog owner (as we assume you are), you probably know your dog well enough to determine when it's time to see the vet.

 Do you eat with your dogs every day?

No, but our dogs eat home-cooked food every day. Linda leans toward Crock-pot meals that can be divided into individual portions and frozen for busy days when she's otherwise too occupied to cook for herself and her dogs. Barbara gives the nod to meat loaves, which she cooks two at a time, slices, and freezes. Either way, there's always good nutritious food in the freezer to be reheated and ready in no time.

Because she has big hunting dogs, Linda also supplements home-cooked food with high-quality kibble dispensed from a creep feeder, which releases the food gradually from a container into a dish. Barbara feeds her dogs a small ration of dry kibble each evening along with the home-cooked food, but most of the time, none of the dogs really wants the kibble. Who can blame them? If you had to decide between a four-star dinner and a bowl of puffed rice, which would you choose?

 And what about exercise?

You may have noticed that virtually every diet book recommends exercise as an essential component of a healthy lifestyle, and we certainly agree. So, in addition to feeding your dog well, do make sure that he has a chance to run free for at least half an hour three times a week. Take him to a park, a dog run, or anywhere he can be both safe and off-leash. Then let him just act like a dog until he's tired. And, please, take plenty of water so he doesn't get dehydrated.

TWO

Every Dog Has His Day— Beginning with a Good Breakfast

When you're lounging about on a weekend and enjoying a special breakfast, there's no reason you should be eating alone—or with mere humans. Any dog worth his keep will love to join you for one of these tasty treats, and he won't be looking over your shoulder and giving you the answers while you're trying to do the Sunday crossword puzzle.

Breakfast Ham-and-Egg Loaf with Chard

This dish is a great company dish that Barbara often serves for brunch at the ranch. Her dogs always come out from under the porch when they get their first whiff. If she wants to serve it for supper, she tarts it up just a bit—the dogs are so easily bored—sometimes turning it into a quiche.

MAKES 4 TO 6 SERVINGS

1 pound Swiss chard

2 large eggs

1/2 cup buttermilk

2 tablespoons olive oil or unsalted butter

1 cup fine whole-wheat bread crumbs

kosher salt and freshly ground black pepper to taste

1 (1/2-pound) ham steak, cubed

2 hard-boiled eggs, sliced, for garnish

Preheat the oven to 375° F. Spray a 9 x 5 x 3–inch loaf pan with non-stick cooking spray.

Trim and discard the stems from the Swiss chard and rinse the leaves very well. Drain and steam in a vegetable steamer or simmer in a small amount of boiling water just until tender, about 10 minutes. Drain well, then cut into chiffonade by stacking the leaves, rolling them up like a fat cigar, and slicing them into ½-inch-wide ribbons.

In a large bowl, combine the eggs, buttermilk, oil or butter, bread crumbs, salt, and pepper and mix well. Add the cooked chard and the ham, and combine the ingredients. Pour the mixture into the prepared pan, cover with foil, and set the loaf pan inside a larger pan on the middle rack of the oven. Fill the outer pan with enough boiling water to come halfway up the sides of the loaf pan. Bake for 25 minutes, or until firm. Cool on a rack. Unmold the loaf and garnish with the sliced eggs.

Sunday Special Quiche

Prepare the loaf mixture as directed above. Line a 12-inch pie or quiche pan with pie dough or thawed frozen puff pastry. Pour the chard mixture into the dough or puff pastry. Bake as above and garnish with the egg slices.

Zucchini Frittata

A frittata is an Italian omelet that can be served hot off the stove or at room temperature. This one is delicious for breakfast or as a great, quick dinner for you and your pooch. It keeps hair shiny and skin supple for both of you. But can you wag your tail?

MAKES 4 SERVINGS

2 tablespoons olive oil

2 medium zucchini, cut into ¼-inch-thick rounds

2 cloves garlic, peeled and smashed

2 brown mushrooms, sliced

½ teaspoon kosher salt

¼ teaspoon crushed red pepper

8 large eggs

2 tablespoons water

4 ounces crumbled goat cheese

¼ cup basil leaves, cut into thin strips

Preheat the oven to 400° F.

Heat the oil in a large, ovenproof skillet and sauté the zucchini, garlic, and mushrooms over medium-high heat until the vegetables begin to brown on the edges, about 5 minutes. Add half the salt and all of the pepper, and cook 30 seconds more. Transfer to a bowl and set aside.

Do not wash out the skillet. Break the eggs into a second bowl and whisk in the remaining salt and the water. Pour the eggs into the skillet and turn the heat to medium-low. Cook without stirring until the eggs are set on the bottom, about 2 minutes. Top with the cooked vegetables, sprinkle with the cheese, and continue cooking until the edges are set and are beginning to puff. Transfer the skillet to the oven and bake about 8 minutes or just until the top is golden brown.

Cut the frittata into wedges and serve hot or at room temperature, garnished with the basil.

Pumpkin Craisin Muffins

Yes, we know that dogs need their vitamins. Pumpkin is an unparalleled source of beta-carotene, a powerful antioxidant that converts to vitamin A in the body to promote good circulation, as well as a healthy heart, eyes, and lungs. The additional presence of alpha-carotene, which interacts with other key nutrients and may help to slow the biological effects of aging in both you and your dog, makes pumpkin a real nutritional standout.

MAKES 12 MUFFINS

MUFFINS:

1½ cups whole-wheat pastry flour

1 cup uncooked old-fashioned rolled oats

½ cup firmly packed dark brown sugar

2 tablespoons dry milk

1 tablespoon baking powder

1½ teaspoons ground cinnamon

½ teaspoon baking soda

½ teaspoon kosher salt

1 cup canned pumpkin puree

¾ cup water

⅓ cup olive oil

1 large egg

½ cup craisins (sweetened, dried cranberries)

STREUSEL TOPPING:

¾ cup uncooked old-fashioned rolled oats

1 tablespoon dark brown sugar

1 tablespoon butter, softened

⅛ teaspoon pumpkin pie spice OR cinnamon

Preheat the oven to 400° F. Line 12 muffin cups with paper liners and spray them with Pam for Baking or Baker's Joy.

Combine the flour, oats, sugar, dry milk, baking powder, cinnamon, baking soda, and salt in a large bowl.

Make a well in the center of the muffin mixture and add the pumpkin, water, oil, and egg. Stir to combine, then stir in the craisins. Transfer the batter to the prepared muffin cups, using about ⅓ cup of batter for each muffin.

In a small bowl, stir together the streusel ingredients.

Sprinkle the streusel evenly on top of the muffins and bake in the preheated oven about 20 minutes or until golden. Cool in the pan to room temperature.

The muffins may be frozen in zip-close bags and thawed to room temperature for serving.

Pure Bread Pudding

Here's a lazy-day brunch dish for those Sundays when you want to read the paper and let your pooch snooze at the foot of the bed before you're up and about. The recipe can be doubled and baked in two loaf pans. Freeze the second one for next Sunday.

MAKES 2 SERVINGS

2 cups high-quality whole-wheat or multigrain bread cubes

1 cup whole milk

1 large egg

¼ cup honey

pinch of crumbled dried seaweed, sea kelp, or sea vegetable (see page 3)

1 tablespoon unsalted butter

Preheat the oven to 350° F. Spray a 9 x 9–inch baking pan with non-stick cooking spray.

Arrange the bread cubes in the pan in a single layer and toast them in the oven about 5 minutes or until golden brown. Cool them in the pan set on a rack. Heat the milk in the microwave for 3 minutes or on the stovetop just until it begins to simmer. Beat the egg until foamy, then whisk in the hot milk, honey, and seaweed. Stir in the butter.

Pour the milk mixture over the bread cubes and let them soak for about 15 minutes or in the refrigerator overnight. Bake in the preheated oven about 25 minutes or until golden brown. Let the bread pudding stand a few minutes before serving. Cut into bite-sized squares for your dog(s).

I wonder if other dogs think poodles are members of a weird religious cult.

—Rita Rudner

Blue Cheese Omelet

Animals never miss breakfast if they have a choice. Serve this omelet over a toasted English muffin for a great Sunday brunch or even an easy dinner. Just remember to break Fido's muffin into pieces before you put the egg on top; otherwise, you may not be pleased with his method of ripping and tearing apart the bread.

MAKES 2 SERVINGS

4 large eggs
4 tablespoons whole milk
1/2 teaspoon kosher salt
2 tablespoons butter
crumbled blue cheese to taste

Break the eggs into a bowl, add the milk and salt, and beat lightly.

Melt the butter in a skillet over medium heat until bubbly, being careful not to let it burn. Pour in the egg mixture, and cook until shiny on the top, tipping the pan and lifting the cooked egg with a spatula to let the raw egg run under the cooked egg. Sprinkle the top with the blue cheese, fold the omelet in half, and slide it out onto a warm platter.

Did you ever walk into a room and forget why you walked in? I think that is how dogs spend their lives.—Sue Murphy

Whole-Wheat Patty Cakes

Great for kids and dogs, these old-fashioned patty cakes are easy to make and irresistible to eat out of hand.

MAKES 24 SILVER-DOLLAR-SIZED CAKES

2 cups whole-wheat flour, plus additional as needed

1/2 cup warm water or buttermilk

1 tablespoon honey or molasses

1/4 teaspoon kosher salt

2 teaspoons extra-virgin olive oil

Preheat oven to 400° F. Spray a baking sheet with nonstick cooking spray.

Place the 2 cups of flour in a dry skillet and heat until the flour begins to give off an aroma and turn golden on the edges, about 2 minutes. Transfer it to a food processor. Add the water or buttermilk, honey or molasses, salt, and oil, and process until the dough forms a ball. Set it aside to rest for 30 minutes.

Sprinkle the countertop with a bit of flour and pat walnut-sized pieces of dough out into flat cakes the size of silver dollars.

Transfer the cakes to the prepared baking sheet. Bake until brown on the edges, about 25 minutes. Cool on a rack and serve like cookies to be eaten out of hand.

The cakes will keep, stored in an airtight tin, for up to three months.

Corn Bread Quiche

Being a Southerner, Barbara loves corn bread. Her Yankee dog kids love it, too, which is just fine with Barbara because she knows it's good for them. We both serve this with freshly sliced tomatoes and red onions for the humans only (see Appendix A) and a side dish of fresh green beans for everyone. The dogs like their beans cut up and put right on top of their corn bread. Applesauce is also very good with this dish.

MAKES TWO 9-INCH QUICHES

1 (6-ounce) package corn bread mix

1/2 cup seeded and chopped red bell pepper

1/2 cup seeded and chopped green bell pepper

1 cup shredded baby carrots

1 cup frozen green peas, thawed and drained well

1/2 cup cooked bacon bits*

Preheat the oven to 425° F. Spray two 9-inch quiche pans with non-stick cooking spray.

Prepare the corn bread batter according to package directions and pour half into each of the prepared pans. Mix together the peppers, carrots, and peas, and spread them over the corn bread batter. Sprinkle with the bacon bits. Using a spatula, gently press the bacon bits into the mixture. Bake the quiches in the preheated oven for 15 to 20 minutes or until golden. Do not overcook.

Serve one quiche and freeze the other for another meal.

***Note:** Bacon bits are sold in jars at the supermarket. Just be sure you don't buy the ones that are artificial.

Mama's Mush with Bacon

The Italians call this polenta, but in the South we call it mush. The leftovers can be turned into a loaf pan, refrigerated, then later sliced and fried for supper. Now that's a real hush puppy. Whether for breakfast or dinner, both man and beast like a fried egg to accompany their mush.

MAKES 6 CUPS

1/2 cup finely chopped bacon (about 4 slices)

1 clove garlic, peeled and minced

5 cups low-salt chicken broth

1 cup frozen corn kernels, thawed

1 cup polenta (coarse cornmeal), NOT the quick-cooking kind

1 cup grated fontina cheese (about 3 ounces)

1/4 cup freshly grated parmigiano-regianno cheese

2 tablespoons chopped fresh parsley

salt and freshly ground black pepper to taste

Sauté the chopped bacon in a large heavy skillet over medium-high heat until crisp, about 8 minutes. Using a slotted spoon, transfer the bacon to a bowl. Pour off all but 2 tablespoons of the drippings from the pan. Add the garlic to the skillet and sauté until golden brown, about 30 seconds. Add the chicken broth, corn, and the reserved bacon; bring to a boil. Gradually add the cornmeal, whisking constantly. Cook, stirring frequently, until the polenta is soft and thick, about 20 minutes. Add the fontina and the parmigiano-regianno cheese, stirring until melted, about 2 minutes. Stir in the chopped parsley, season to taste with the salt and pepper, and serve hot.

Scratch a dog and you'll find a permanent job.—Franklin Jones

Flaked Oats or Barley

Oats and barley are vital canine foods. They are good sources of iron and help to cleanse the intestine of impurities. And as if that weren't enough, this healthy, hearty breakfast food requires no cooking at all.

MAKES 2 SERVINGS

1 (3-ounce) package flaked oats (sometimes labeled instant oats) or barley, preferably organic

enough water or vegetable broth to cover the oats

3 tablespoons shredded carrots

3 tablespoons fresh green peas

1 teaspoon honey

1 tablespoon fresh lemon juice

2 tablespoons chopped walnuts

Soak the oats or barley overnight in the water or broth. In the morning, stir in the vegetables, honey, lemon juice, and walnuts. Serve to both man and beast.

Variation: You can also add finely chopped apple and stir in a dollop of plain yogurt before serving.

Sausage Cheese Grits

We love Jimmy Dean sausage, but you can use any kind you like. If we pick up the extra-spicy version, the dogs require long drafts of cool water from the nearest source—even if it's the toilet—so we try to be considerate and choose a "mild" variety.

MAKES 16 SQUARES

6 cups water

1½ cups quick-cooking grits

2¾ cups grated Monterey Jack cheese (about ¾ pound)

2 tablespoons unsalted butter

salt and freshly ground black pepper to taste

¾ pound bulk fresh sausage (not spicy—see note above)

1 tablespoon vegetable oil

1 large green or red bell pepper, seeded and finely chopped

6 large eggs

2 teaspoons Worcestershire sauce

Preheat the oven to 350° F. Butter an 8 x 8–inch ovenproof glass baking dish.

Bring the water to a boil in a large, heavy saucepan. Slowly stir in the grits and simmer, covered, stirring occasionally, until firm and cooked through, about 7 minutes. Stir in 1 ½ cups of the cheese, the butter, the salt and pepper to taste. Continue stirring until the cheese is melted, then spread the mixture in the prepared baking dish.

In a heavy skillet, brown the sausage over moderate heat, stirring and breaking up the lumps. When cooked through, transfer it with a slotted spoon to paper towels to drain. Pour off the fat from the pan, add the oil, and cook the bell pepper over moderately low heat, stirring, about 5 minutes until softened.

In a bowl, whisk together the eggs, Worcestershire sauce, and salt to taste. Stir in the sausage and pepper, and spread the mixture over the grits.

Sprinkle with the remaining cheese and bake on the middle rack of the preheated oven for 30 to 35 minutes or until the eggs are firm. Cut into 2-inch squares and serve hot or at room temperature.

Growly Good Granola

It is positively silly to watch dogs eat granola. They just munch and munch and munch. How much to feed them? Use your judgment. Ours would eat themselves into a stupor if we let them, but we start off our big hunting dogs with a cup. Serve it dry or with a little milk—it's equally good either way.

MAKES ABOUT 12 CUPS

3 cups old-fashioned rolled oats

2 cups cracked wheat

2 cups bran flakes

2 cups sliced almonds

1¹/₂ cups sweetened flaked coconut

¹/₄ teaspoon salt

¹/₂ cup vegetable oil

1 teaspoon pure vanilla extract

¹/₂ cup honey

1 cup dried cranberries

1 cup sunflower seeds

Put the oven rack in the middle position and preheat the oven to 375° F. Line a large shallow baking pan with foil and spray it with nonstick cooking spray or coat it with vegetable oil.

In a large mixing bowl, toss together the oats, wheat, bran flakes, almonds, coconut, and salt. Whisk together the oil, vanilla, and honey, and stir into the oat mixture until all the ingredients are well coated.

Spread the mixture in the prepared baking pan and bake, stirring occasionally, until golden brown, about 25 to 30 minutes. Stir in the cranberries and sunflower seeds and return to the oven for 3 minutes. Cool the granola completely in the pan set on a rack. The granola will keep up to a month stored in an airtight tin.

THREE

Bone Appetite— Hors d'Oeuvres for Hounds

Dogs may not know how to pronounce the French word for appetizers, but they sure know them when they see them. And, if left to their own devices, dogs will graze across a wide range of finger and paw foods. Our dogs love dim sum and sushi. They are crazy for Buffalo wings and mozzarella sticks. But perhaps their favorites are cheeses. Once, when Linda invited a few friends in for wine and cheese, her guests arrived bearing a noble bottle, which she took to the kitchen to uncork. By the time she returned to the living room, Aften, her 85-pound Muensterlander, had wolfed down $14 worth of a fine French cheese left on the coffee table. The lesson here is to lay out your spread above your dog's nose level and serve him one piece at a time. Otherwise you may have an overfed hound on your hands.

Beggar's Purses

All dogs are beggars, but with these tasty treats they'll think they're eating like kings (or queens).

MAKES 64 BITE-SIZED MOUTHWATERING PUFFS

1 (6-ounce) can Italian tuna in olive oil (do not drain)

6 cloves garlic, peeled and smashed

1/2 cup drained, finely chopped black olives (about 3 ounces)

2 tablespoons drained capers, rinsed and chopped

1 tablespoon minced parsley

1 (17 1/4-ounce) package frozen puff pastry sheets, thawed

Line a baking sheet with parchment paper or a silicone-impregnated mat (e.g., Silpat). Preheat the oven to 400° F.

Stir together the tuna in oil, garlic, olives, capers, and parsley.

Flour a countertop surface and roll out the puff pastry to approximately 12 inches square. Cut into 1½-inch squares. Using a teaspoon, place the filling into the middle of each square. Pull up the corners and pinch shut to make a filled "purse."

Transfer the purses to the prepared baking sheet and bake in the preheated oven about 20 minutes or until golden brown. Serve on a silver tray while purses are still warm.

Retro Rumaki for Rover's Cocktail Party

Who can blame dogs for being sentimental? The fifties were the ne plus ultra *for cocktail parties. Along with pigs in blankets, rumaki ruled as the martinis flowed. Some traditions deserve a comeback, so the next time you're serving drinks in the company of dogs, bring on the rumaki. Just remember to remove the wooden toothpicks before feeding the pups.*

MAKES 24 TENDER BITES

MARINADE:

¼ cup soy sauce

1 teaspoon fresh minced ginger

2 cloves garlic, peeled and smashed

2 tablespoons dry sherry

¾ pound chicken livers, lobes separated

12 whole water chestnuts, halved

12 slices bacon, halved crosswise

Preheat the broiler.

In a medium bowl, combine soy sauce, ginger, garlic, and sherry.

Add the chicken livers and water chestnuts. Turn to coat, and marinate in the refrigerator for at least ½ hour or up to 4 hours.

Drain the livers and water chestnuts. Place 1 chicken liver piece and 1 chestnut piece in the center of each half slice of bacon. Roll up and secure with a toothpick. Transfer the rumaki to a broiler pan or shallow baking pan, and broil about 5 or 6 inches from the heat for 10 to 15 minutes or until the bacon is crisp. Alternatively, you can bake the appetizers in a 375° F oven for 20 to 25 minutes. Serve hot.

No animal should ever jump up on the dining-room furniture unless absolutely certain that he can hold his own in the conversation.

—Fran Lebowitz

Cheddar Chomps

Both you and your dog will love these pretty golden flaky biscuits. If you and your pooch are invited to a party, take a bottle of wine for the hostess and a box of these for her pet.

MAKES 50 SMALL BISCUITS

2 large eggs

1/4 cup chicken broth

2 cups whole-wheat flour

1 1/3 cups shredded sharp Cheddar cheese

3 cloves garlic, peeled and finely chopped

1/2 cup olive oil

1 tablespoon honey mixed with 1 tablespoon water

Preheat oven to 400° F. Line a baking sheet with foil.

Whisk the eggs and chicken broth together and set aside.

Combine the flour, cheese, garlic, and oil in the bowl of a food processor fitted with a steel blade. Pulse 6 seconds. Scrape down the sides of the bowl and pulse another 5 seconds. The mixture should have the texture of coarse meal. With the machine running, drizzle in the egg mixture, mixing just until the dough forms a ball. Do not overmix the dough.

Divide the dough in half and knead each half on a floured surface for 3 minutes. Roll out each piece to 1/4-inch thickness.

Cut with a small round biscuit cutter and transfer the biscuits to the prepared baking sheet.

Bake in the preheated oven for about 15 minutes or until the tops are golden brown. Remove the biscuits from the oven and turn them over. Return the biscuits to the oven and bake another 10 minutes. Remove the biscuits from the oven and brush the tops with the honey-and-water mixture.

Cool the biscuits on a rack and store, loosely covered, at room temperature.

Barbara's First Dog

My relationships with dogs began when I was six years old. Tubby was my very first "own" dog. We lived in the country and my grandmother lived in town. After school one day, I went to my grandmother's house, as I often did after school, to wait for my mother to pick me up. But this day was different; it was a glorious day in my life.

Mrs. Hicks was my grandmother's best friend, who lived directly across the street from her. When I went to my grandmother's that day, she told me that a female dog had arrived at Mrs. Hicks's house during the night and had given birth to seven pups. Would I like to go and see them? To this day, I can still see those tiny balls of wiggles. It was love at first sight. For the next six weeks, I begged, cried, pitched fits, and behaved as if I were possessed—which I was.

All this time, Mrs. Hicks was wondering aloud how she was ever going to "get rid" of all those dogs. Well, I knew about city people who took animals to the country and dumped them, and so I intended to take charge of the situation. My solution was to keep Tubby and find homes for his six littermates. I put the six puppies in a box and began my journey across our very small West Texas farm and ranch town, stopping at the homes of my friends and schoolmates. Needless to say, by dusk all six puppies were in the hands and homes of ecstatic children and not-so-ecstatic mothers.

And, speaking of mothers, my own wasn't too pleased when she found out about the newest addition to our household. In fact, she said it was "out of the question," pointing out that, like most farm and ranch people, we already had "big" dogs bred to do country work, and there was no place in our lives for small dogs. But I just planted my feet and gave her my now-famous "back off, it's a done deal" stare. She did, and told me many times through the following years that she knew I was not going home without my Tubby. In fact, for many years I hardly went anywhere without him. He was my eyes and ears, my playmate, and my confidant. I taught him things he never knew real dogs in the real world didn't do.

I baked and we ate mud pies. After some terrible wrecks, we perfected riding my bicycle together—he in front of me, his little back legs straight out, away from the spokes and pedals, his front paws curled around the handle bars, hanging on for dear life.

And now you know how it all began and why it has never stopped. After Tubby I've owned and loved:

Sampson, 13 years
Pero, 11 years
Joshua, was stolen
Brodie, 17 years
Brigit, hit by a car
Burt, 13½ years
Bree, 9 years
Jilly, almost 17 years
Duggan, 13 years
Dooley, 14 years at present
Dickie, 14 years at present

Dooley doesn't see too well and Dickie is losing her hearing. Between them, I sometimes think they make one whole dog. Actually they are really in very good shape. It's the way we eat. As I write this, I am preparing our dinner of organic chicken cooked in fresh garlic, sea kelp, and water. It will be served with fresh green beans and steamed carrots. I will sprinkle a few barley flakes on theirs.

Chicken "Brownies"

This gives new meaning to the word brownie, but they sure are tasty.

MAKES 36 SMALL BROWNIES

1 cup cooked chicken

1¹/₂ cups reduced-sodium
chicken broth

2 large eggs

¹/₈ teaspoon dried, flaked
garlic

¹/₈ teaspoon cayenne pepper

1³/₄ cups cornmeal

2¹/₄ cups whole-wheat flour

Preheat the oven to 400° F. Spray a 9-inch square baking dish with Pam for Baking or Baker's Joy.

Combine the chicken, broth, and eggs in a food processor and puree. Add the garlic, cayenne, cornmeal, and flour, and pulse to make a soft dough. Pour into the prepared pan and smooth the top. Bake in the preheated oven for 20 minutes or until brownies begin to pull away from the sides of the pan. Cool on a rack, then cut into squares.

Turkey Polenta Pups

These make tasty appetizers for both humans and canines. Our dogs have voted over and over for Paul Newman's marinara sauce. Actually, we think they just have a crush on Paul. We prefer Classico ourselves. Use whatever brand you prefer.

MAKES 8 SERVINGS

1 tablespoon olive oil

1/2 pound ground turkey

1 clove garlic, peeled and minced

3 tablespoons chopped green bell pepper

3 tablespoons chopped red bell pepper

salt and pepper to taste

1 (16-ounce) tube ready-cooked polenta, sliced into 16 1/2-inch-thick rounds

1/2 cup marinara sauce

1 cup shredded mozzarella cheese

Preheat the oven to 425° F. Spray 8 individual ramekins with non-stick cooking spray.

Heat the oil in a skillet, add the turkey, and cook about 3 minutes, until it is just beginning to brown. Add the garlic and green and red bell peppers, and cook 2 more minutes. Season to taste with salt and pepper.

Place 1 polenta round in the bottom of each ramekin. Top with 1 tablespoon of cooked meat, 1 teaspoon of marinara sauce, and 1 tablespoon of mozzarella cheese. Top with a second polenta round and 2 more tablespoons of cheese.

Set the ramekins on a cookie sheet to catch spills, and bake them on the center rack of the preheated oven until bubbly and hot, about 15 minutes. Garnish each "pup" with 1 tablespoon of marinara sauce. Serve warm in the ramekins or, for the dogs, turned out into a bowl.

Barking Burgers

Believe us when we say Fido will not be the only one barking after tasting these little cocktail treats. You and your guests will love them, too. Especially the Russian wolfhounds.

MAKES ABOUT 12 BABY BURGERS

1 pound 90-percent-lean ground sirloin

2 tablespoons sour cream

1 tablespoon black caviar or salmon roe

6 mini-bagels, sliced horizontally (optional)

12 small lettuce leaves (optional)

Combine all the ingredients and shape into patties the size of silver dollars.

Broil or pan fry to desired doneness.

Serve on a mini-bagel half with a little piece of lettuce under the burger or on a toothpick with a tiny dot of aioli (see recipe, next page) on top. Be sure to remove the toothpicks before feeding these to your dogs.

Not Carnegie, Vanderbilt, and Astor together could have raised money enough to buy a quarter share in my little dog.

—Ernest Thompson Seton

Aioli

In addition to topping Barking Burgers, this aioli is also good as a dip for raw vegetables. Our dogs particularly like it with organic baby carrots.

2 cloves garlic, peeled

pinch of salt

1 large egg yolk

2 teaspoons fresh lemon juice

1/2 teaspoon Dijon mustard

1/3 cup high-quality, fruity extra-virgin olive oil

salt and pepper to taste

Mince and mash the garlic and salt to a paste with the side of a large heavy knife or in a mortar with a pestle. In a bowl, whisk together the egg yolk, lemon juice, and mustard. Add the oil a few drops at a time, whisking constantly until all is incorporated and the mixture is emulsified. (If the mixture separates, stop adding oil and continue whisking until it comes together, then resume adding oil.)

Whisk in the garlic paste and season with the salt and pepper.

If the aioli is too thick, whisk in 1 or 2 drops of water.

Refrigerate, covered, until ready to use. The aioli will keep in the refrigerator for up to two days.

Chow Bella Burger Bites

Both your dog and your best friend—even if they are not one and the same—will love these tasty, quick-to-fix little nibbles.

MAKES 12 BITE-SIZED BURGERS

1 pound 90-percent-lean ground beef

1 large egg

1/2 cup mixed cooked vegetables, such as carrots, peas, beans, and potatoes, diced

1 tablespoon crumbled dried seaweed, sea kelp, or sea vegetable (see page 3)

1/2 teaspoon kosher salt

1/4 teaspoon freshly ground black pepper

1 teaspoon garlic flakes

vegetable oil or cooking spray for the pan

In a bowl, combine all the ingredients and mix thoroughly.

Form into a dozen small patties and cook to your preferred doneness over medium heat in a skillet lightly filmed with oil or cooking spray. Spear with toothpicks for humans; just feed them by hand to dogs.

Simply Shrimp Cocktails

Got a plastic martini glass? Our dogs like to slurp up their cocktail party nibbles from a footed dish. Yes, Fido will want to chomp down the tails, and that's perfectly okay, but you may want to remove them before eating your own shrimp.

MAKES 4 SERVINGS

1 slice lemon, plus additional for garnish

4 sprigs parsley

1 clove garlic, peeled and smashed

1 teaspoon crumbled dried seaweed, sea kelp, or sea vegetable (see page 3)

1 pound large shrimp, shelled and deveined

1 quart water

1 cup shredded iceberg lettuce

4 teaspoons cocktail sauce, store-bought or homemade

Combine the lemon slice, parsley, garlic, seaweed, shrimp, and water in a medium pot and bring to a boil. Cook just until the shrimp turn pink, about 3 minutes. Cool in the water.

When the water is cool, drain the shrimp and serve them by hooking them on the edges of 4 martini glasses filled with shredded lettuce. Squeeze the lemon over the shrimp and add a teaspoon of cocktail sauce to the middle of each glass.

Simple Sushi Hand Rolls

Once you get the rice cooked and the seaweed ready, you can fill the hand rolls with your dog's favorite filling. Our dogs like ham and cucumbers. So do we. Or we sometimes make California rolls. Ours have avocado, crabmeat, cucumber, and sesame seeds, but dogs can't have avocado (it's on the ASPCA danger list), so we make some without it just for them. The possibilities are limited only to your time and imagination. If you have access to sushi-grade tuna, dogs love that. And salmon. Just cut all fillings into julienne slices and layer them into the roll. Add a sprinkling of sesame seeds, either natural or black, and you have an appetizer everybody will lap up.

MAKES 24 ROLLS

1/4 cup Japanese rice vinegar

1/4 cup sugar

1/4 teaspoon kosher salt

1 cup uncooked short-grain rice

12 sheets of dried seaweed (see page 3)

deli ham strips

cucumber, cut into sticks

radish sprouts

Combine the rice vinegar, sugar, and salt in a small pan and simmer until the sugar dissolves. Remove from the heat and set aside to cool.

Wash and cook the rice according to package directions.

Sprinkle half of the vinegar sauce over the hot cooked rice and mix gently. Taste, and add more vinegar sauce if desired.

Cut a sheet of seaweed in half to make a rectangle about 3 x 4 inches. Place a seaweed rectangle on your left hand and top with a small amount of rice. Wet the fingers of your right hand, and flatten the rice to make a small rectangle. Add ham, cucumber, and radish sprouts (or another filling of your choice). Wrap the seaweed around the filling, rolling from left to right. Continue until all the ingredients are used up. Serve immediately.

Doggie Dumplings

Serve these to your four-legged friends as slurpy treats, or treat your two-legged guests to a bowl of dumplings (toothpicks on the side) with their drinks.

MAKES 20 SMALL DUMPLINGS

1 cup stone-ground cornmeal

1 cup whole-wheat pancake mix

1/2 teaspoon crumbled dried seaweed, sea kelp, or sea vegetable (see page 3)

1 teaspoon honey

2 cups chicken broth

Combine all ingredients except the chicken broth and mix in just enough cold water to form a stiff dough. Pat into flat cakes about 2 inches in diameter and 1/2 inch thick.

Bring the chicken broth to a boil in a small saucepan, then reduce the heat to a simmer.

Drop in the dumplings, cover, and simmer until they rise to the top, about 20 minutes.

Serve the dumplings in a deep bowl along with the broth.

FOUR

Salad Days

Dogs love raw vegetables. If you don't believe us, just turn any dog loose in the backyard and watch him crop grass as efficiently as a sheep. Dogs know they need the roughage and chlorophyll, so it's only a short leap to get them to eat salads that are good for them and for you, too. Our dogs are particularly fond of sweet organic baby carrots as well as many fruits.

Here's what Barbara has to say about feeding dogs these healthy, organic treats:

In my house, we call salad fixings "treats to end all treats." I've trained all my dogs to love cucumbers, carrots, radishes, and mushrooms. This is accomplished by calling them into the kitchen for their "treats." I take a bite, then give them a bite. They love to share.

I usually steam carrots lightly and slice them into pieces appropriate for the size of the dog. If I'm using them along with other ingredients in a recipe, I always peel them before slicing, grating, or chopping. If serving them raw, I shred them finely.

Grilled Flank Steak and Portobello Mushrooms over Cucumber and Radish Salad

Why deprive your dog of the tantalizing flavor and aroma of grilled steak and portobello mushrooms served over gently dressed cucumbers and radishes? I guarantee that the minute your pet gets a whiff, he will grace you with a look of undying love. The addition of chopped radish tops to the salad will also add a welcome cold crunch that dogs seem to crave.

1 (1½ to 2 pound) flank steak

2 large portobello mushrooms, cleaned

MARINADE:

½ cup extra-virgin olive oil

½ cup red wine

¼ cup soy sauce

¼ cup honey

4 cloves garlic, peeled and minced

1 teaspoon EACH: cracked black peppercorns, oregano, and thyme

SALAD:

1 bunch radishes with tops, washed and drained, bulbs and tops chopped separately

1 small English cucumber, peeled and sliced paper-thin

2 tablespoons chopped walnuts

grated zest of 1 orange

DRESSING:

juice of 1 orange

1 teaspoon Dijon mustard

¼ cup extra-virgin olive oil

kosher salt and freshly ground black pepper to taste

MAKES 6 SERVINGS

Lay the steak and mushrooms in a large glass dish. Whisk the marinade ingredients together and pour over the meat and mushrooms. Cover and marinate on the countertop about 30 minutes.

Meanwhile, prepare the vegetables and combine all the ingredients for the dressing.

Heat an indoor or outdoor grill, and grill the steak and mushrooms to medium-rare. Cut them into thin slices.

To serve, toss the radish tops with some of the dressing and make a bed on the bottom of each dog's and human's plate or bowl. Fan the cucumber slices and chopped radishes over the radish tops, and arrange the warm steak and mushroom slices on top. Drizzle with additional dressing, and sprinkle with the walnuts and orange zest. Serve at once.

Beef and Coleslaw Salad

It was perhaps not altogether an accident that our dogs taught us the wisdom of serving cold roast beef with coleslaw. We had cooked their favorite from the Crock-pot—eye round roast—on the same day that we had purchased lovely coleslaw for our own lunch. While our backs were turned, slicing the roast beef, the slavering beasts snaked their long pink silken tongues into the coleslaw and ate about half of it off the countertop. We figured, what the heck? So we divided the remaining slaw among their dishes and ours and arranged the sliced beef on top. The combination is positively inspired. Thank you, faithful gourmands. Your taste is, as usual, impeccable.

MAKES 6 SERVINGS

3 cups cooked eye round roast (see page 68)

3 cups prepared coleslaw

black bread

butter

Slice the beef thin. Place a dollop of slaw in each dog's dish, then fan out the beef slices on top. Do the same for yourself. Or serve with slices of buttered black bread for a totally satisfying lunch.

A well-trained dog will make no attempt to share your lunch. He will just make you feel so guilty that you cannot enjoy it.

—Helen Thompson

Healthy Rice Salad

Our dogs love this recipe, which we adapted from one we found in
Dr. Pitcairn's Complete Guide to Natural Health for Dogs and
Cats, *a reference we turn to frequently. The salad, which combines high-
quality protein with complex carbohydrates, will tempt perfectly healthy dogs
and humans, and will also benefit those who need to watch their protein
intake, e.g., those with a kidney problem.*

*Dr. Pitcairn says to feed your dogs as much as they will eat, but offers
the following quantities as a guide. "This recipe will feed a 10-pound toy
dog for 3 days, or a 40-pound dog for 1 day."*

MAKES 4 CUPS OR 2 TO 3 SERVINGS

**1 clove garlic, peeled and
minced**

**2 tablespoons extra-virgin
olive oil**

**¼ teaspoon kosher salt plus
more salt to taste**

**freshly ground black pepper
to taste**

**¼ pound 90-percent-lean
ground beef**

**2¾ cups hot cooked enriched
white rice**

1 large egg

2 tablespoons minced parsley

2 tablespoons grated carrot

Sauté the garlic in the oil in a large skillet. Add ¼ teaspoon of the
salt and all of the beef, and cook until the meat loses its pink color.
Stir in the hot cooked rice, egg, parsley, and carrot. Toss until the
egg cooks. Serve at room temperature, adjusting the seasonings to
taste with additional salt and the freshly ground pepper.

Sweet Corn and Basmati Rice Salad with Smoked Chicken, Garlic, and Parsley

A Dijon mustard vinaigrette brings all the flavors together. If you can't find basmati rice, long-grain white rice is fine, although some Asian breeds may turn up their noses at the less aromatic rice. We suggest putting newspaper under your dog's bowl when you serve this, as there's certain to be a fair amount of slurping going on. Washable place mats for humans may also be in order.

MAKES 8 SERVINGS

VINAIGRETTE:

2 tablespoons red wine vinegar

1 tablespoon Dijon mustard

1/2 cup extra-virgin olive oil

Salt and freshly ground black pepper to taste

3 large ears yellow corn, husked

1 tablespoon extra-virgin olive oil

2 cloves garlic, peeled and smashed

1 red bell pepper, finely chopped

1 cup chopped smoked deli chicken (about 4 ounces)

1/2 teaspoon kosher salt

freshly ground black pepper to taste

11/2 cups cooked basmati rice

1/4 cup coarsely chopped toasted pecans

1 bunch parsley, stems discarded

To make the vinaigrette, whisk the red wine vinegar and mustard together in a large bowl. Gradually whisk in the oil. Season to taste with the salt and pepper.

Using a sharp knife, cut the corn kernels from the cobs. Heat the oil in a large heavy skillet over medium heat. Add the garlic and sauté 30 seconds. Add the corn kernels and bell pepper and sauté until the corn is crisp-tender, about 5 minutes. Add the chicken, season with the salt and pepper to taste, and stir in the cooked rice.

To compose the salad, toss the corn mixture with the pecans in a large bowl. Add the vinaigrette and parsley, and toss to combine. Serve warm or at room temperature.

Super Chicken Salad

This salad is so easy and so good. Make sandwiches with it for yourself or serve it on a lettuce leaf with fresh bread, wine, fruit, and cheese to top it off. Your dog gets served in a little bowl—no lettuce, no bread, and definitely no wine, poor thing.

MAKES 2 SERVINGS

1¼ cups boneless, skinless, cooked, cooled, and cubed chicken

¼ cup finely chopped celery

¼ cup finely grated carrot

plain low-fat yogurt to taste

3 tablespoons minced parsley

Combine all the ingredients, toss lightly, and serve at once.

Note: Sometimes we add a little curry and turmeric for a curried chicken salad.

One reason the dog has so many friends: He wags his tail instead of his tongue.

—Anonymous

Chopped Salad With Chicken and Couscous

We discovered how much dogs love this salad on a visit to the Hamptons, where a friend served it to the humans on a sunny deck on a summer day. We just happened to put down a plate for the dogs and guess what? They lapped it up, getting buttermilk all over their whiskers and smiling from ear to ear.

MAKES 8 SERVINGS

½ **packed cup fresh basil leaves**

½ **cup mayonnaise**

½ **cup buttermilk**

1 **tablespoon fresh lemon juice**

salt and freshly ground black pepper to taste

¼ **cup grated parmigiano-reggiano cheese**

⅓ **cup dried craisins**

2 **strips crisp-cooked bacon**

⅓ **cup shelled pumpkin seeds**

3 **cups coarsely chopped iceberg lettuce**

1 **cup chopped tomato**

2 **grilled chicken breast halves, diced**

2 **ears corn, cooked, kernels cut from the cob**

1 **(10-ounce) package plain couscous, cooked according to package directions**

Blend the basil leaves and mayonnaise in food processor until smooth.

Gradually blend in the buttermilk and lemon juice. Season dressing to taste with salt and pepper, and set aside while you prepare the salad.

Combine the cheese, craisins, bacon, and pumpkin seeds in a medium bowl.

In a second, larger bowl, toss the lettuce, tomato, chicken, and corn with the couscous. Add the dressing to taste, and top with the pumpkin seed/bacon mixture.

Serve at once.

Sautéed Collard Greens With Bacon and Corn Bread

A long cooking time for collard greens is a Southern tradition. We cut ours into thin ribbons, then sauté them only for 1 minute, which renders them crisp-tender but allows the greens to keep their color and full flavor. Every dog comes out from under the porch for a mess of these collards with bacon. Humans might serve it as a side dish with roast chicken, and a pan of corn bread is always welcome. But all by itself, it makes a great hot salad in the spirit of wilted greens.

MAKES 6 TO 8 SERVINGS

3 pounds collard greens, leaves halved lengthwise, stems and center ribs discarded

2 tablespoons vegetable oil

8 slices thick bacon, chopped

salt and freshly ground black pepper to taste

1 pan cooked corn bread, from a mix or your own favorite recipe (optional)

Stack several collard leaf halves and roll up tightly into a cigar shape. Cut crosswise into very thin slices (no wider than ⅛ inch). Roll and slice the remaining leaves in the same manner.

Heat the oil in a 12-inch heavy skillet over moderately high heat until hot but not smoking. Add the bacon and cook until crisp. Add the collards and toss with tongs just until bright green, about 1 minute. Season with salt and pepper to taste. Serve warm, with some hot corn bread crumbled in if you wish.

Cucumber Salad

Remember the dog days of August, when it's hot and horrible. A cooling cucumber salad is just the ticket to accompany grilled meats—for both of you.

MAKES 3 SERVINGS

1 (1-pound) seedless cucumber, cut into thin rounds

¹/₂ teaspoon sea salt

¹/₂ teaspoon cumin seeds

¹/₂ cup chopped fresh cilantro

¹/₂ cup plain yogurt

Toss the cucumber with the salt in a colander and set it in the sink to drain for 20 minutes, then pat dry.

Toast the cumin seeds in a dry small heavy skillet over low heat, stirring constantly until fragrant and a shade darker, 3 to 4 minutes. Cool on a cutting board, then crush slightly with a rolling pin.

In a bowl, stir together the cucumber, cumin, cilantro, and yogurt. Refrigerate until serving time.

Salad Supper

No reason your pooch should be left out of this let's-clean-out-the-refrigerator meal. After all, what are dogs for if not to help you dispose of leftovers?

MAKES 3 SERVINGS

1½ cups cubed, cooked, cold meat (chicken, roast beef, pork roast, lamb)

¼ cup grated carrot

½ cup almost any leftover veggies or grains (there goes that Chinese take-out rice)

mayonnaise or plain yogurt to moisten

¼ cup chopped parsley

kosher salt and freshly ground black pepper to taste

In a large bowl, combine the meat, carrot, vegetables, mayo or yogurt, and parsley. Season to taste and serve at once. See who cleans his plate first.

If you pick up a starving dog and make him prosperous, he will not bite you; that is the principal difference between a dog and a man.—Mark Twain

Carrot Craisin Salad

Northern Africa contributes this dog- and man-friendly salad. Served with any meat, it's a meal for both of you. Use the food processor to grate the carrots for the quickest results. Cover and store the salad in the fridge up to three days. The flavors just get better and better.

MAKES 4 SERVINGS

1 pound baby carrots, coarsely grated (about 4 cups)

$1/4$ cup extra-virgin olive oil

3 tablespoons fresh lemon juice

$1/4$ cup chopped fresh cilantro

$1/4$ cup craisins

2 to 4 cloves garlic, peeled and mashed or minced

$1/2$ teaspoon ground cumin

$1/4$ teaspoon ground cinnamon

1 teaspoon sweet paprika

pinch of salt

Combine all the ingredients in a large bowl. Cover and marinate in the refrigerator for at least 2 hours. Serve chilled or at room temperature.

FIVE

Chow Down—
The Main Course

Anyone who's ever owned a dog knows that he spends the dinner hour hoping for manna from heaven—a morsel that might fall from the table. Now you can give Rover exactly what he's been dreaming of all his life—a chance to share your meal.

How many times have you cooked something so delicious you were tempted to lick the plate clean? Well, your dog will certainly do that when you serve him one of the delicious and nutritious dishes in this chapter. And if the two of you are eating alone, you might even throw caution to the wind and do the same yourself.

Crock-pot Chicken and Kasha

If you had to pick just one recipe from this book to adopt for daily use, this would be the one to choose. It is delicious, nutritious, and trouble free, and no matter how often you serve it, your dogs will eat it as if they'd never tasted anything so yummy in their lives.

In fact, when Linda goes out of town and boards her dogs in a kennel, she freezes zip-close baggies of this meal to send with them. The kennel master reports that all the other dogs are jealous when they get a whiff of Aften and Ruby's dinner, but that's what happens when you cook for your dogs. Everybody wants to come to their dinner party.

MAKES 8 SERVINGS

1 (3- to 4-pound) package chicken legs and thighs

1 cup kasha, brown rice, barley, or other grain your dog enjoys

1 cup leftover vegetables of your choice (peas, carrots, greens, whatever you have—even leftover green salad works fine)

1 teaspoon Spike (see page 3)

1 teaspoon crumbled dried seaweed, sea kelp, or sea vegetable (see page 3)

3 cups water

Combine all ingredients in a Crock-pot, cover, set on high, and let the stew cook all day. At the end of the day, transfer it to a 9 x 12 x 3–inch pan and pull the meat from the bones. Stir all the ingredients together and serve. Freeze leftovers for another meal.

Chicken Soup for Me and My Dog

Chicken soup gives comfort to me and my pets. Made in the Crock-pot, it goes together in five minutes and will burble away while I'm at work. Thirty minutes before serving, I can add pasta, rice, or barley and whatever vegetables I have in the fridge. Carrots and/or peas are always favorites, and garlic is a must.

Leftovers can be bagged and frozen for that inevitable rainy day, or simply refrigerated to serve the next day. None of us objects to eating the same thing two days in a row—especially when it tastes this good.

MAKES 8 SERVINGS

1 (4-pound) package chicken pieces OR 1 whole chicken

1 teaspoon crumbled dried seaweed, sea kelp, or sea vegetable (see page 3)

6 cloves garlic, peeled and smashed

kosher salt and freshly ground black pepper to taste

1 (16-ounce) can chicken broth

3 ribs celery, chopped

3 carrots, scraped and cut into rounds

1 cup brown rice OR pasta OR barley

Season the chicken with the seaweed, garlic, and salt and pepper to taste. Place it in the Crock-pot, and add the broth and enough water to cover. Cook on high until tender, about 5 hours. Add the celery, carrots, and rice (or other leftover veggies) and cook for 45 minutes more. Remove bones from the chicken. Adjust the seasonings and serve.

Hola! Adobo Chicken

I promise, the bitter orange and garlic flavors in this adobo seasoning along with the crispy skin will leave both you and your dogs in a postprandial stupor. This chicken is great with rice and beans and/or a simple salad. (Our dogs request cooling cucumbers in vinegar with this dish, and we recommend fresh pineapple for dessert.)

MAKES ABOUT 4 SERVINGS

4 chicken legs with thighs (about 3 pounds)

Dry adobo seasoning (we use Goya brand)

Heat the oven to 350° F.

Arrange the chicken pieces on a baking sheet and sprinkle generously with adobo seasoning. Roast in the oven for 30 to 45 minutes, until the meat is tender and the juices run clear when the thigh is pierced with a fork. Cool a bit, then tear the meat apart with two forks, discard bones, and serve.

Here are the surprising (or not-so-surprising) results of a survey of dog owners in the United States done by the American Pet Association.

- 31,589,887 dog owners said they bought Christmas gifts for their dog
- 9,843,962 dog owners said they celebrate their dog's birthday in the following ways:
  - Give the dog a special treat: 4,567,598
  - Make the dog a special meal: 1,978,636
  - Give the dog a cake: 1,850,665
  - Give the dog a new toy: 1,801,445
  - Give the dog ice cream: 1,102,524
  - Give the dog a new bone: 964,708
  - Sing happy birthday to the dog: 698,921
  - Give a birthday party with other dog guests: 659,545
  - Take the dog to a favorite place: 393,758
  - Take doggie portrait photographs: 216,567

Chicken Paprika

Paprika is made from a blend of ground red chilies, and can range from hot to smoky to sweet. With nine times the vitamin C of citrus, it's an easy way for both dogs and humans to load up on this essential vitamin. In Florida zoos, paprika is put into the flamingos' food to guarantee their dazzling plumage color. You'll also find it added to dog biscuits for color and flavor. Holistic vets prescribe vitamin C for dogs with hip dysplasia. So why not make sure your dog gets his fill in a tasty supper dish?

MAKES 6 SERVINGS

3 whole skinless chicken breasts (about 1¹/₂ pounds)

kosher salt and freshly ground black pepper to taste

1 tablespoon olive oil

1 tablespoon Hungarian sweet paprika

2 large portobello mushrooms, sliced

1 cup chicken broth

1 cup sour cream

1 roasted red pepper, thinly sliced

2 cups wide egg noodles, cooked according to package directions

¹/₄ cup minced fresh Italian parsley

Season the chicken with the salt and pepper. Heat the oil in a heavy skillet, add the chicken, and brown on all sides. Stir in the paprika (careful, it burns) and mushrooms. Add the broth, reduce heat, cover, and simmer until the chicken is tender, about 45 minutes. Transfer the chicken to a cutting board and slice it thin, discarding bones. Stir the sour cream into the pan juices and add the red pepper. Bring to a boil and return the chicken to the pan to reheat briefly. Toss with the cooked noodles, garnish with the parsley, and serve at once.

Good Gravy

If you ever had any illusion that you could con dogs into eating icky, chemical-filled gravy out of a can, they are likely to set you straight with one withering glance. Our dogs insist on the real thing poured over their ration of rice, and once you've tasted it, you will, too. It's a bit of trouble, but worth it. Freeze the leftovers in ice cube trays and you'll always have some on hand to tempt picky eaters, both canine and human.

MAKES 3 CUPS

1/2 cup all-purpose flour

1/2 cup extra-virgin olive oil

2 large carrots, scraped and cut into chunks

2 large celery stalks, broken into pieces

2 cloves garlic, peeled and smashed

1 teaspoon whole peppercorns

handful of fresh parsley sprigs

2 teaspoons dried thyme

1 teaspoon dried sage

1 tablespoon crumbled dry seaweed, sea kelp, or sea vegetable (see page 3)

2 (10-ounce) cans chicken broth

2 cups water

neck and giblets from 1 chicken

1/2 cup dry vermouth

salt and freshly ground black pepper to taste

Stir the flour in a skillet over medium-high heat until it begins to brown and yields a toasty aroma. Add the oil and cook just a couple of minutes until golden brown. Stir in the carrots, celery, garlic, peppercorns, parsley, thyme, sage, and seaweed. Cook down, stirring over medium-low heat for about 5 minutes to make a gorgeous golden roux. Add the chicken broth and stir vigorously until the mixture is smooth. Add the water, chicken neck, and giblets. Simmer for about 2 hours to cook the meat and reduce the liquid by half. Discard bones. Add the vermouth, remove the gravy from the heat, and strain it. (Your dogs will relish what's left behind in the strainer.) Season to taste with the salt and pepper.

Bulldog Drumsticks

Tryptophan-rich turkey is a flavorful choice for restless dogs. One good turkey meal and they'll snooze away the day. Come to think of it, so will you. Peel all the bone and cartilage away from the meat and make sure the dogs can't get to them. Our dogs are masters of the dumpster dive in the kitchen, and we certainly don't want them to come across turkey or other poultry bones that could puncture their gut. Never forget that your dog's nose is a thousand times more sensitive than your own. Be careful how you discard foods you don't want him to have.

MAKES 2 SERVINGS

3 tablespoons extra-virgin olive oil

3 tablespoons fresh lemon juice

1/8 teaspoon garlic powder

2 turkey legs (about 1 pound)

1 tablespoon honey

1 tablespoon Spike (see page 3)

Preheat the broiler. Combine the olive oil, lemon juice, and garlic powder. Put the turkey legs in a deep bowl and pour the mixture over them. Cover loosely and marinate in the refrigerator for 2 hours. Remove the legs from the marinade and arrange them on a foil-lined broiler pan.

Mix the honey with 1 tablespoon of the marinade. Brush the legs with half the honey mixture, sprinkle them with the Spike, and broil about 25 minutes until golden brown. Turn the legs, baste with the remaining honey mixture, and cook another 25 minutes or until the meat is tender and golden. Remove all bones and cartilage and serve.

Turkey Roulade with Basil and Roasted Peppers

Our dogs have a highly developed aesthetic sense, and appreciate food that is well presented. When they saw their favorite turkey breast rolled around colorful roasted red peppers and brilliant green basil, then grilled, they clapped their paws. Sometimes, we grill the roll over charcoal, but on bad-weather days, we use a grill pan in the kitchen and simply turn the meat with tongs until it's cooked through. Either way, it's ready in less than 25 minutes, and that's a good thing. You know what a short attention span dogs have.

MAKES ABOUT 6 SERVINGS

1 boneless half turkey breast (about 2 pounds)

kosher salt and freshly ground black pepper to taste

2 teaspoons extra-virgin olive oil

1 roasted red pepper

2 cups large basil leaves

SAUCE:

1 cup sour cream

1/3 cup finely chopped fresh basil leaves

juice and grated zest of 1 large lemon

Preheat an outdoor grill or a grill pan. If using charcoal, light a chimney of charcoal until the ashes are grayish-white, then spread the charcoal into an even layer in the bottom of the grill.

Place a sheet of plastic wrap over the turkey breast half and pound it to a uniform ½-inch thickness. Season to taste with the salt and pepper. Moisten the meat with half the olive oil. Lay the red pepper, then the basil, on the meat, and roll it into a tight cigar. Tie it up with kitchen string and drizzle the remaining oil over the meat. Grill, turning as needed until the roll is golden brown on all sides and the internal temperature has reached 150 degrees at the thickest part. Cool on a rack. Snip the string and cut the roll into ½-inch-thick slices.

To make the sauce, stir together the sour cream, chopped basil leaves, and grated lemon zest and juice. Put a dollop of sauce atop each slice of turkey roll before serving.

Turkey Meatballs over Pasta

Don't forget a generous grating of parmigiano-reggiano cheese on top of everybody's dish. Dogs love this cheese. Freeze any remaining meatballs for another day.

MAKES 50 SMALL MEATBALLS (ABOUT THE SIZE OF LARGE MARBLES)

2 tablespoons extra-virgin olive oil, plus additional for cooking meatballs

6 cloves garlic, peeled and smashed

3 celery stalks, finely chopped

1 cup chopped kale or spinach

1 pound ground turkey

1 cup fresh whole-wheat bread crumbs*

2 tablespoons minced sun-dried tomatoes

¼ cup sour cream

1 large egg

2 teaspoons dried oregano

salt and freshly ground black pepper to taste

cooked pasta of your choice

your favorite marinara sauce

freshly grated parmigiano-reggiano cheese

Heat 2 tablespoons of the oil in a 10-inch skillet. Add the garlic, celery, and kale, and sauté until the celery is soft.

Meanwhile, in a large bowl, combine the turkey, bread crumbs, tomatoes, sour cream, egg, oregano, and salt and pepper. Add the sautéed veggies and mix thoroughly. Form the mixture into balls about 1 inch in diameter, the size of large marbles. A small ice cream scoop works well for this.

Transfer the meatballs to a tray lined with waxed paper and refrigerate for at least 15 minutes.

Rinse out the skillet in which you sautéed the vegetables and film the bottom with fresh olive oil. Add the meatballs and cook over medium heat, turning frequently to brown on all sides. Drain on paper towels as they're done.

To serve the dog, make a mound of cooked pasta, add a couple of meatballs, sprinkle with grated parmigiano-reggiano, and serve. For humans, heat your favorite marinara, add pasta, toss, then add a few meatballs. Top with cheese and serve.

*Note: To make quick bread crumbs, tear up 3 to 4 slices of good, whole-grain bread, and pulse in the food processor to fine crumbs. For buttered bread crumbs, toss with melted butter after pulsing.

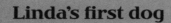

Linda's first dog

I was born in 1939 on a ranch in Kansas. My mother's mother was sick with cancer and was living in the Texas panhandle. At the same time, my mother's marriage was falling apart. So we went home to my grandmother's house in Hereford, Texas. As World War II progressed, they put a POW camp in Hereford and filled it with Italian prisoners. The reason they chose Hereford was because it was such a flat and feature-less plain, they knew that the prisoners would have nowhere to go if they escaped.

My mother got divorced. My grandmother got sicker, and eventu-ally my mother began to date some of the military police (MPs) from the camp. One night, one of her beaus came bearing a gift for me. It was a little white shorthaired dog with a black ring around one eye and around the base of its tail—a lot like the dog you see in the Target ads these days.

It seems that the dog had been smuggled all the way from Italy by one of the prisoners, but once it was discovered, the guards wouldn't let him keep it. I, an only child who spent most of her time alone in the house with a sick grandmother, named the dog Billy John Lee West. Soon, we discovered a few things about the dog.

First of all, he spoke only Italian. And second, he liked spaghetti more than any other food in the world. We had to train that dog to eat hush puppies and biscuits with milk gravy. But he seemed to like sausage right away and soon discovered the joy of pork chops. We told him he'd become an American.

Eventually my mother remarried, and her new husband was a re-luctant dog lover, but we soon had him trained, too. Once, after the war, in our brand-new robin's-egg-blue Plymouth with the scratchy seats, we were going on vacation to see the horse races in Ruidoso, New Mexico. My friend Virginia and I smuggled Billy along hidden in a blanket. That short trip was a piece of cake for such an experienced stowaway. The one problem was that he would do his business only on a particular kind of grass, so we spent the entire vacation hunting for motels with Bermuda grass for the dog.

When I went away to college, Billy was still alive and riding in the car with my stepdad wherever he went. That fine Italian dog made us a family. And since then, I have always had a dog.

Spaghetti Squares with Fresh Mozzarella and Tomato

If you cut these small, they can also be passed and eaten out of hand as an hors d'oeuvre.

MAKES 4 MAIN COURSE SERVINGS
MAY BE DOUBLED OR TRIPLED AS NEEDED

extra-virgin olive oil

8 ounces thin spaghetti or linguini

2 large eggs, lightly beaten

1/2 cup whole milk

4 ounces tomato sauce of your choice

1 teaspoon dry Italian seasoning

1/2 teaspoon garlic flakes

1/4 teaspoon cayenne pepper

1/2 cup water

4 ounces low-fat fresh mozzarella cheese, shredded

Preheat the oven to 350° F. Coat a 9 x 13–inch baking pan with the olive oil.

Cook the spaghetti in a large pot of boiling, barely salted water. Drain and transfer to the prepared pan.

Whisk together the eggs, milk, tomato sauce, seasoning, garlic, cayenne, and water. Pour over the spaghetti in the pan. Sprinkle with the cheese, and bake for 45 minutes. Serve warm or at room temperature, cut into squares.

I've seen a look in dogs' eyes, a quickly vanishing look of amazed contempt, and I am convinced that basically dogs think humans are nuts.—John Steinbeck

Lamb Shish Kebabs

The Persians, who invented the kebab, probably never fed it to their dogs, but more's the pity. Dogs love it. When we make it, we also string tomato quarters on alternate skewers and serve the people both meat and tomatoes. For the dogs, skip the tomatoes. They won't mind.

MAKES 8 SERVINGS

4 cloves garlic, peeled and smashed

1 teaspoon kosher salt

$1/2$ teaspoon freshly ground black pepper

$1/2$ cup fresh lime juice

$1/4$ teaspoon ground saffron threads, dissolved in 2 tablespoons of hot water

2 pounds boneless lean leg of lamb cut in $1^1/2$-inch cubes

olive oil

lemon juice

crumbled dried seaweed, sea kelp, or sea vegetable (see page 3)

1 recipe Canine Kasha (recipe follows)

In a bowl, combine the garlic, salt, pepper, lime juice, and saffron threads. Place the lamb cubes in a single layer on a flat dish and pour the marinade over the meat. Cover and refrigerate overnight, turning once or twice.

When you're ready to cook, preheat the charcoal grill or broiler. String the lamb cubes on flat metal skewers, leaving space between pieces so that they cook on all sides. Combine the olive oil and lemon juice, brush it on the meat, and sprinkle the meat with the seaweed.

Broil or grill the skewers over the charcoal, turning them often to brown them evenly, until crusty brown on the outside and pink inside, about 5 minutes. Remove from the skewers and serve over the kasha.

Canine Kasha

Kasha is nothing more than buckwheat groats, a whole-grain product popular in the Middle and Far East, as well as in Russia, that's healthy for both people and pets.

MAKES 3 SERVINGS

1 cup chicken broth

1 cup water

3 tablespoons extra-virgin olive oil

1 cup kasha (buckwheat groats)

1 large egg, lightly beaten

1 clove garlic, peeled and minced

1 red bell pepper, seeded and chopped

1 zucchini, scrubbed, halved lengthwise, and cut into 1/4-inch-thick slices

kosher salt and freshly ground black pepper to taste

In a large saucepan, combine the broth and water with 1 tablespoon of the oil and bring to a boil.

In a bowl, combine the kasha and the egg, stirring to coat the kasha well. Transfer the kasha mixture to a deep skillet with a lid, and cook it over moderately high heat, stirring and breaking up any lumps, for 2 to 4 minutes or until the grains are separated. Add the broth mixture slowly to the skillet, cover, and reduce heat. Cook until the kasha is tender and all the liquid is absorbed, about 15 minutes.

While the kasha is cooking, heat the remaining two tablespoons of oil in a medium skillet and sauté the garlic and pepper over low heat, stirring until the vegetables are soft. Add the zucchini and the salt and pepper to taste. Increase the heat to medium-high and cook about 3 minutes or just until the zucchini is tender. Stir the vegetables into the kasha and serve under the lamb.

North Carolina Pork Sandwiches

The Crock-pot is never more welcome than when it comes to cooking a pork shoulder. Our dogs lie on the kitchen floor for hours, dreaming, inhaling, and waiting for this most luscious of dinners. Remember, this is rich food, so don't overfeed them.

MAKES 12 PEOPLE SERVINGS

SAUCE:

2 cups apple cider vinegar

1/2 cup ketchup

2 tablespoons Worcestershire sauce

1 tablespoon (packed) light brown sugar

1 tablespoon Dijon mustard

1 teaspoon salt

1 teaspoon crushed red pepper flakes

1/2 teaspoon black pepper

4 cloves garlic, peeled and smashed

1 untrimmed boneless pork shoulder (about 3–4 pounds)

12 hamburger buns, split

Combine all the ingredients except the pork and buns in a large heavy saucepan.

Simmer over medium heat for 5 minutes. Remove from the heat, cover, and let stand for 2 hours.

Put the pork shoulder in a Crock-pot, cover, and roast on high for 3 hours, or until the skin is golden and crisp. Transfer the meat to a cutting board and make several crosswise slashes in the meat with a sharp knife, being careful not to cut all the way through. Brush the meat with 1 cup of the sauce, return the meat to the Crock-pot, and continue cooking about an hour longer or until a meat thermometer inserted into the center registers 165° F.

Place the meat on a cutting board and remove any tough rind and bones. Chop the meat into bite-sized pieces.

Transfer the meat to large bowl and add enough of the remaining sauce to moisten it. Put the bottom of a bun on a plate or in a bowl. Top with a portion of the pork and then the other half of the bun. Pass additional sauce on the side or, for the dogs, just spoon some more over the tops of their buns.

Roasted Pork Chops

There is nothing wrong with an occasional serving of pork for your pets. Just remember—no pork bones ever, and the pork must be thoroughly cooked.

MAKES 2 SERVINGS

2 thick center-cut loin pork chops (about 1¹/2 pounds)

¹/2 lemon, peeled and sliced

¹/4 cup bread crumbs

³/4 teaspoon sea salt or crumbled dried seaweed, sea kelp, or sea vegetable (see page 3)

2 tablespoons soft butter

juice of 1 lemon

Preheat the oven to 400° F.

Place the pork chops in a greased baking dish, top each with a slice of lemon, and sprinkle each with the bread crumbs and sea salt.

Dot the pork chops with the butter and add a squeeze of lemon juice to each. Roast in the preheated oven 30 minutes or until cooked through but not dry.

Remove the meat from the bone before serving to dogs.

You can say any foolish thing to a dog, and the dog will give you a look that says, "My God, you're right! I never would've thought of that!"—Dave Barry

Woof Raisers

Here's a burger with a vitamin and mineral boost. Plus, we always punch ours up with garlic. Add garlic as often as you like to anything and everything you serve to your dogs. Little woofers love it, and it will keep both of you flea-free!

MAKES 2 SERVINGS

1/2 **pound 90-percent-lean ground beef**

1 cup Swiss chard, cut into thin ribbons

1/2 **cup cooked, crumbled turkey bacon**

1 large egg, beaten

1/8 **teaspoon crumbled dried seaweed, sea kelp, or sea vegetable (see page 3)**

1 tablespoon minced parsley

2 cloves garlic, peeled and smashed

Combine all ingredients in a large bowl and mix thoroughly. Shape into 2 patties and brown on both sides in a heavy skillet. Serve yours on a toasted bun if you wish. Break the dog's up with a fork and serve it with or without the bun.

Quickie Burgers

If you're cooking for two, just make all four patties and freeze two for another day.

MAKES 4 PATTIES

1 pound ground sirloin

1 large beaten egg

$^1/_3$ cup tiny fresh green peas or $^1/_3$ cup shredded carrots

$^1/_3$ cup whole kernel corn

$^1/_3$ cup finely chopped celery

$^1/_2$ teaspoon crumbled dried seaweed, sea kelp, or sea vegetable (see page 3)

$^1/_2$ teaspoon garlic powder

In a large bowl, combine all ingredients and mix well. Shape into four patties and broil or sauté in a skillet to medium rare. Serve at once.

Beef Teriyappi

Teriyaki is a combination of two Japanese words, teri, *meaning "luster," and* yaki, *meaning "broil." We just call this dish yappi for short because the aroma of the beef cooking in the pan makes the dogs go completely nuts.*

For humans, a mere 3 ounces of lean beef is an excellent source of 5 basic nutrients: protein, zinc, vitamin B_{12}, selenium, and phosphorus, as well as a good source of niacin, vitamin B_6, iron, and riboflavin. This nutritional powerhouse of a meal can be served in really small amounts to small dogs to keep them healthy. And remember, sharing is a good thing.

MAKES 5 SERVINGS

1¹/₂ pounds flank steak

2 tablespoons vegetable oil

1 tablespoon sweet rice wine OR sake

1 tablespoon soy sauce

¹/₂ teaspoon brown sugar

1 clove garlic, peeled and smashed

1 lime, sliced thin

2 cups cooked wild rice

Cut the beef into ¹/₄-inch-thick slices and pound lightly with a mallet. Combine the oil, rice wine, soy sauce, sugar, garlic, and lime slices in a large bowl, and add the beef. Cover and marinate in the refrigerator for about 1 hour, turning the meat twice to be sure it is well coated.

Remove the beef from the marinade and broil or grill it until just medium rare, under 5 minutes. Serve on a bed of wild rice.

Eye Round Roast for Rover

For flavor, it's hard to top the eye round roast of beef. The only problem is that it's so lean it can be tough. Cooking it in a Crock-pot ensures that it will be tender enough to satisfy both you and your dog. We usually cook potatoes in the microwave and serve them split with the cooking juices from the bottom of the pot. A small salad on the side (or underneath for the pooch), and you'll have a simple supper you'll both adore.

MAKES ABOUT 6 SERVINGS

1 eye round beef roast (about 3 pounds)

salt and freshly ground black pepper to taste

6 cloves garlic, peeled and smashed

Season the roast to taste with the salt and pepper. Toss the garlic cloves into the bottom of a Crock-pot and add the meat. Cover and cook on high for about 4 hours, or until the meat is tender. Serve the meat in thin slices along with a baked potato or rice. Leftovers are great the next day in salads or sandwiches.

There is no psychiatrist in the world like a puppy licking your face.—Bern Williams

Puppy Sitter de Veau

You know how it is. It's Saturday night, you're all alone with your best friend, and the telephone doesn't ring. What better way to spend the evening than cuddled up before the fire eating a delicate dinner? You'll want champagne. Your pal will probably prefer deep drafts from the water bowl. For entertainment, may we suggest Animal Planet?

MAKES 2 SERVINGS

2 thin slices veal scallopini (about 1/2 pound)

1 tablespoon melted butter

1/2 cup sliced crimini mushrooms

1/2 cup chicken broth

2 cups cooked brown rice

2 tablespoons minced Italian parsley

Brush one side of each veal slice with the melted butter. Spread the mushrooms evenly on the buttered side of the meat, roll up, and tie with string or secure with a wooden toothpick. Be sure to remove the toothpicks before serving your dog.

Arrange the veal in a buttered, heavy skillet, add the broth, and braise, covered, over low heat until the meat is fork-tender, about 25 minutes. Serve on a bed of the rice, sprinkled with the parsley. We like a side of French-cut green beans with this dish.

Veal Breast with Veggies

Anything you can throw in a Crock-pot and cook all day without watching is a winner in our book. Dogs love veal breast—fat, bones, and all—so we often make this simple stew and enjoy it along with them. Veal bones are as safe as beef bones for dogs.

MAKES 8 SERVINGS

1 veal breast (about 1¹/₂ pounds)

kosher salt and freshly ground black pepper to taste

1 teaspoon crumbled dried seaweed, sea kelp, or sea vegetable (see page 3)

1 cup baby carrots

3 ribs celery, finely chopped

4 cloves garlic, peeled and smashed

1 cup barley

Combine all ingredients in a Crock-pot and add water to cover. Cook on high until tender, about 5 hours.

Transfer the meat to a cutting board and chop into bite-sized pieces, then replace in the Crock-pot and stir with the pan juices, vegetables, and grain. Taste and adjust the seasonings with salt and pepper, if necessary. Spoon into the dog's dish and your own soup bowl. Save any leftovers in zip-close bags and refrigerate for up to 3 days or freeze for up to 6 months.

Roasted Veal Breast Stuffed with Spinach and Sun-dried Tomatoes

Veal breast has long been beloved by traditional cooks because it is full of flavor and inexpensive to boot. Believe us, this is good enough for company—say, when your best friend wants to come for dinner and bring Fifi, her Lhasa apso, who will, as you'll see, lap this up.

MAKES 8 SERVINGS

1 (4- to 5-pound) bone-in veal breast

kosher salt and freshly ground black pepper to taste

STUFFING:

1/2 pound ground veal or beef

2 cups fresh bread crumbs (see note, page 57)

1 (6-ounce) package baby spinach, microwaved for 1 minute

1/4 cup minced sun-dried tomatoes

2 large eggs

2 tablespoons dried or fresh parsley

2 tablespoons minced garlic

1/8 teaspoon ground nutmeg

PAN VEGETABLES:

4 large carrots, halved, then cut into 2-inch pieces

2 celery ribs, finely chopped

2 cups chicken broth, plus additional as needed

1 cup dry vermouth

Preheat the oven to 425° F.

Lay the veal breast flat with the rough side up. Where the meat seems to fold over itself, form a pocket by separating the layers with your fingers. Open it only on one side, and season it to taste with the salt and pepper.

In a bowl, combine the ground meat, bread crumbs, spinach, tomatoes, eggs, parsley, garlic, and nutmeg. Season to taste with salt and pepper, and mix with your hands to form a soft stuffing.

Pack the stuffing into the pocket of the breast, and roll and secure it with wooden skewers. Be sure to remove the skewers before serving your dog.

Lay the stuffed breast in a large roaster. Add the carrots, celery, 2 cups of broth, and the vermouth to the pan. Place the roaster on the middle shelf of the preheated oven and roast 20 minutes. Reduce the heat to 350° F and continue roasting until the veal is very tender, about 2 hours, basting every 30 minutes with the pan juices and adding additional broth as needed to keep about 1 inch of liquid in the pan. When done, remove the roast from the oven and let it rest about 20 minutes before slicing.

To serve the pooch, mash the carrots with a fork and cut the meat into bite-sized pieces. For the folks, simply slice and serve. Mmm. Good for man and dog.

Simple Poached Salmon

Don't be afraid to feed your dogs salmon. They'll love it, and it's good for them. Just be sure to pick out all the bones before serving.

In case you're worried about "salmon poisoning," which can be fatal to dogs, you should know that it comes from a bacteria in the fish guts, not from the flesh of the fish. So, if you're taking your dog for an outing, avoid lakes or streams where fishermen might be catching fish and gutting them on the spot. That's where "salmon poisoning" comes from. And actually, many freshwater fish have this same bacteria. It's really insidious in that the symptoms don't show up for about 2 weeks, and the dog goes from looking perfectly fine to being deathly ill in a matter of hours. Run to the vet if you suspect that your dog has gotten into fish guts. Linda's bad boy dog Asher got salmon poisoning from turning over the neighbor's trash can. We saved that big, sweet, powerful, naughty, 90-pound Muensterlander only because I had an alert dog training husband and we had an alert vet who figured out what was wrong with the dog quickly and shot him full of antibiotics.

MAKES ABOUT 6 SERVINGS

6 (6-ounce) salmon fillets

3 cups vegetable stock OR water acidulated with lemon slices

Wrap the fish fillets in several thicknesses of cheesecloth, leaving long ends to hang over the edges of the pan. Bring the stock to a boil in a large, shallow pan that will hold the fish in a single layer and lower the salmon into it. If you have a rack that will fit in the pan, that is ideal. If not, you must be careful not to break up the fish when removing it from the liquid. Reduce the heat to a gentle simmer and cook the fish covered until a thermometer plunged into the thickest part of the meat registers 160° F.

Serve the poached salmon hot with lemon butter or cold with a simple mayonnaise flavored with chopped watercress (our dogs' fave). You can also top the fish with chopped hard-cooked eggs and minced parsley. You'll love these garnishes as much as your pooch will, and if either one of you has had a flea problem lately, the parsley will run them right off.

Buttered Scallops

This dish is so delicious that it will leave not only the dogs but you howling for more. If your market sells diver scallops, by all means buy them. They've been dry cured, and retain the absolute best flavor.

MAKES 2 TO 3 SERVINGS

2 tablespoons unsalted butter, plus additional for the pan

1/2 teaspoon minced garlic

1/4 teaspoon kosher salt

1 pound fresh or quick-frozen scallops

Lightly butter a shallow baking pan. Combine the 2 tablespoons butter, the garlic, and the salt in a small bowl. Place the scallops in the baking pan and brush with half the butter mixture. Broil or pan-fry 3 to 4 minutes, or until lightly browned around the edges. Turn the scallops, brush with the remaining butter mixture, and cook the second side, no more than 2 to 3 minutes. Serve hot. We like this with rice pilaf and a side of spinach.

Rover Dover Sole

Our dogs love fish, and yours will, too. Just take care not to overcook the delicate sole. Remember to remove all the bones. It's ready almost before you are.

MAKES 2 SERVINGS

2 sole fillets (about ¾ pound total)

½ cup light cream

1½ tablespoons white whole-wheat flour*

½ teaspoon kosher salt

1 tablespoon extra-virgin olive oil

3 tablespoons butter

juice of 2 lemons

lemon wedges, for garnish

Dip the fillets in salted water, then drain and pat dry on a paper towel. Pour the cream into a deep pie plate. In a separate dish, mix the flour and salt. Dip fillets in the cream, then in the salted flour. Shake away any excess and set the fillet aside while you heat the pan.

Preheat the pan dry, then add the oil and 1 tablespoon of the butter. When the butter foams, carefully lay in the fillets. Cook just until they begin to turn brown around the edges, no more than 2 to 3 minutes. Carefully turn the fish and brown on the other side.

Turn the golden-brown fillets out onto a warmed serving platter.

Melt the remaining butter in a small dish in the microwave. Mix in the lemon juice and pour over the fish. Garnish with the lemon wedges and serve at once.

Your little dog friends will appreciate a side dish of warm rice—perhaps left over from your last trip to a Chinese restaurant.

*White whole-wheat flour is a new product that performs like white flour but has the nutrition of whole wheat. It is available from King Arthur.

Pekingese Duck

Dogs love duck. Barbara's miniature poodle, Bridget, would stand in the kitchen and point as Barbara prepared this dish. Bridget took the same stance with quail, dove, and pheasant, but never with chicken. Smart dog. Remember to remove the bones before serving your pet.

MAKES 3 TO 4 SERVINGS

1 small Long Island duckling (about 1$\frac{1}{2}$ pounds)

1 large egg yolk

3 tablespoons mild honey

1 teaspoon powdered garlic

1 tablespoon olive oil

$\frac{1}{4}$ cup fresh orange juice

1 orange, peeled and sliced thin

1 teaspoon unsalted butter

Halve the duck by cutting through the backbone with kitchen shears.

Beat the egg yolk well, then add the honey, garlic, oil, and orange juice, and stir until well mixed. Place the duck, cut sides down, in the pan, brush with the marinade, and broil 6 inches away from the heat for about 20 minutes, basting often with additional marinade.

Turn the duck over, baste it again, and cook 10 minutes longer. Then flip it again, baste it with the marinade, move it closer to the heat source, and finish cooking skin side up, for 5 to 10 minutes.

While the duck is cooking, sauté the orange slices in the butter for about 5 minutes and serve them on top of the duck.

Mom's Macaroni and Cheese

Our editor, Erin Moore, grew up in the Florida Keys with a veterinarian father and an expert mac-and-cheese-making mom. The dogs they inevitably inherited from the hospital always gave four paws up to mac and cheese. Here's a classic version that has gone to the dogs. Leftovers can be frozen or will hold in the refrigerator for 2 to 3 days, and neither dogs nor human folks object to eating this twice.

MAKES 8 SERVINGS

1 pound elbow macaroni, cooked according to package directions

1 recipe Cheesy Béchamel Sauce (recipe follows)

1 cup grated sharp Cheddar cheese

1 cup fresh buttered bread crumbs (see note, page 57)

Preheat the oven to 375° F. Butter a 3-quart casserole.

Put the cooked macaroni into the casserole, pour the Béchamel Sauce over it, and mix gently with a fork. Sprinkle the grated cheese evenly over the top, and spread the crumbs over the cheese. Bake, uncovered, until the top is golden and the sauce is bubbling, about 30 minutes.

Cheesy Béchamel Sauce

4 tablespoons butter

4 tablespoons flour

2¹/₂ cups milk, heated

salt and freshly ground black pepper to taste

1 cup grated sharp Cheddar cheese

pinch of cayenne pepper

Melt the butter in a heavy-bottomed saucepan. Stir in the flour and cook, stirring constantly, for about 2 minutes until the paste cooks and bubbles a bit, but don't let it brown. Add the hot milk, continuing to stir as the sauce thickens. Bring it to a boil. Add the salt and pepper to taste, lower the heat, and cook, stirring, for 2 to 3 minutes more. Remove from the heat. (At this point, the sauce can be cooled for later use. Cover it with waxed paper or pour a film of milk over it to prevent a skin from forming. Reheat when ready to use.) Stir in the cheese and cayenne during the last 2 minutes of cooking.

Meat Loaf Madness

We all love meat loaf. It makes us think of our mothers' kitchens, and now we make it any way we can think of and share it with our own four-legged kids.

We often make two meat loaves at a time—one to eat hot for dinner and then slice for sandwiches, the other to slice and freeze in individual portions for the days when we need something quick and nutritious for all of us.

The following meat loaf recipes make use of minced meat from a variety of sources: beef, veal, pork, and tuna. We love them all because they're convenient and really easy to prepare.

Grandmother's Meat loaf

Barbara's grandmother always served this with fluffy mashed potatoes, freshly snapped green beans in the summer, and Del Monte canned beans in the winter. Fresh relish, a dish of green onions, sliced tomatoes, and the small crunch of radishes and cucumbers were side dish staples. Grandmother didn't even have to think the word organic. *Everything just* was. *We* have to *make a special effort to buy organic, but we think it's worth it.*

It was Barbara's job to scrape the leftovers into the dogs' dishes way back when. Even today, this is probably still her dog's favorite meal.

MAKES 6 TO 8 SERVINGS

1 pound 90-percent-lean ground beef

1/2 pound ground veal

1/2 pound ground pork

2 large eggs

1/2 cup fine whole-wheat bread crumbs

3/4 cup chopped parsley

1/2 teaspoon dried oregano

1/2 teaspoon dried basil

1/4 cup coarsely chopped green bell pepper

1 1/2 teaspoons kosher or sea salt

1/2 teaspoon black pepper

3–4 strips uncooked bacon

Preheat the oven to 350° F.

Combine all the ingredients except the bacon in a large bowl and blend with a light hand. Form the mixture into a loaf, set it on a rack in a 10-inch baking pan, and cover it with the bacon slices. Bake uncovered in the preheated oven for about 1 1/2 hours or until the loaf is firm and the bacon is browned. Cool slightly before slicing. Freeze leftover slices in zip-close bags for another day.

Ms. B's Holiday Turkey Loaf

For Thanksgiving Barbara always buys a really big turkey to be sure she has plenty of leftovers for making this loaf. The dogs really seem to get the tryptophan effect, because after one generous serving, they snooze all afternoon. Don't forget to pass the cranberry relish to your two-legged diners.

MAKES 4 TO 6 SERVINGS

1 1/2 pounds cooked turkey, mostly white meat, ground or finely chopped

2 cups leftover cooked stuffing

2 large eggs, lightly beaten

1/2 cup finely ground fresh bread crumbs (see note, page 57)

1/2 cup leftover gravy, sour cream, or a mixture of both, plus additional as needed

1 teaspoon dried thyme, OR sage, OR poultry seasoning

kosher salt and freshly ground black pepper to taste

Preheat oven to 350° F. Spray a 9 x 5 x 3–inch loaf pan with Pam or other pan-release agent.

In a large bowl, thoroughly combine all the ingredients. If the stuffing is dry (for example, if it was baked outside the turkey as mine is), you may need to moisten it by adding additional gravy or sour cream.

Press the mixture into the prepared pan and bake in the preheated oven 45 minutes to 1 hour or until brown and firm. Cool slightly and slice thin.

Italian Tuna Roll

Think of this as a lace-curtain meat loaf. Your dogs may break into arias over it, because it's that delicious. Make the effort to locate Italian tuna packed in olive oil for the most nutritious, delicious version. We buy Progresso.

The recipe is easier than it sounds, so don't be afraid to try it. You'll thank us, and your dogs will definitely thank you.

MAKES 4 TO 6 SERVINGS

1 pound fresh spinach OR 1 (10-ounce) package frozen whole-leaf spinach, thawed

1 (6-ounce) can Italian tuna in olive oil

4 anchovies, drained

1/2 cup good-quality dried whole-wheat bread crumbs

1/2 cup buttermilk

2 large eggs, lightly beaten

1/2 cup freshly grated parmigiano-reggiano cheese

1/2 teaspoon dried oregano

kosher salt and freshly ground black pepper to taste

2 tablespoons fresh lemon juice

grated zest of 1 lemon

lemon slices, for garnish

If using fresh spinach, wash it and cook it in a large pot of boiling water about 8 to 9 minutes, then plunge into ice water to set the color, drain, and cool. Strain out the excess liquid by squeezing it between your fingers, and chop fine. For frozen, simply thaw and squeeze out the excess liquid. Transfer the spinach to a large bowl.

Drain the tuna, add the anchovies, and chop fine. Mix with the spinach in the bowl.

Soak the bread crumbs in the buttermilk for 5 minutes or so. Pour off the excess milk and add the bread crumbs to the tuna mixture. Add the eggs, cheese, oregano, salt, pepper, lemon juice, and zest. Combine well and form the mixture into a roll about 3 inches in diameter. Wrap the roll in several layers of cheesecloth, and tie at both ends. Be sure the ends of the cheesecloth are long enough to hang over the ends of the pan so that you can use them to lift the loaf out once it is cooked. Wet them, and fold them over the lid to prevent them from burning.

Place the roll in a lidded flameproof baking dish that is just large enough to hold it and add boiling water to cover. Cover the dish with the lid. Bring to a boil over high heat, then lower the heat and simmer for 30 minutes.

Remove the roll from the pot by lifting it with the ends of the cheesecloth. Cool slightly, remove the cloth, and cool the roll completely. Slice and garnish with the lemon slices.

Clean-Out-the-Fridge Loaf

Barbara likes to make this on Fridays to use up all leftovers in her fridge. Remember that the six elements of any meat loaf are meat, bread, binding agent, moistener, flavorings, and vegetables. Decide which group each of your leftovers belongs to, and follow the basic recipe.

MAKES 6 TO 8 SERVINGS

2 pounds or 3 cups meat (beef, pork, chicken, turkey, lamb, or veal) ground or chopped in the food processor, all bones removed

1 cup fine bread crumbs

1 large egg

1/2 cup chicken stock or other moistener

2 cloves peeled garlic or other flavoring agent

1/2 teaspoon salt-free Spike (see page 3)

1/4 teaspoon crumbled dried seaweed, sea kelp, or sea vegetable (see page 3)

2 cups cooked vegetables such as peas, shredded carrots, finely chopped broccoli, or string beans, or a combination of vegetables

Preheat oven to 350° F.

Combine all the ingredients in a large bowl and mix very well. Transfer the mixture to a 9 x 5 x 3–inch oiled loaf pan and bake in the preheated oven for 45 minutes to 1 hour.

Lamb Loaf

If you can't get a butcher to grind lamb, buy shoulder chops, remove the meat from the bones, and grind it yourself in a food processor. If you have Afghan hounds, Pharaoh hounds, or other "dogs of the desert," the Middle-Eastern flavors in this loaf may cause them to get a faraway look in their eyes as they remember their land of origin.

MAKES 6 TO 8 SERVINGS

1 cup dried green lentils

1/2 teaspoon plus 1 tablespoon crumbled dried seaweed, sea kelp, or sea vegetable (see page 3)

1 tablespoon olive oil

2 cups fresh spinach

1 cup fine, dry whole-wheat bread crumbs

1 pound ground lamb

2 finely chopped Granny Smith apples

1 teaspoon cinnamon

1/4 teaspoon cloves

1 tablespoon fresh lemon juice

1/2 teaspoon powdered ginger

2 large eggs

1 tablespoon Spike (see page 3)

1/2 cups pine nuts

Preheat the oven to 350° F. Spray a 9 x 5 x 3–inch loaf pan with cooking spray. Cook the lentils in a medium pot with 2 cups of water and 1/2 teaspoon of the seaweed until soft, about 30 minutes. Set aside to cool.

Heat the oil in a 10-inch skillet, add the spinach, and sauté it until limp, about 5 minutes.

Transfer the lentils and spinach to a large bowl and add all the remaining ingredients. Mix well with your hands and press the mixture into the prepared pan.

Bake in the preheated oven for about 1 hour or until the meat is cooked through and the juices run clear. Cool at least 15 minutes, cut into thick slices, and serve. (Leftovers, if there are any, can be frozen in individual portions for another day.)

Mutt Man Meat Loaf

Many generations of settlers in the Midwest brought with them a taste for simple, hearty foods. This meat loaf is one of those dishes. Good for the mutts and good for the man. We use organic meats and make the corn bread from a mix. If you wish, you can add one of the sauces that follow this recipe to "tart up" the people servings. Just remember that the sauces are for people only, not canines.

MAKES 6 TO 8 SERVINGS

1 tablespoon canola oil

2 cloves garlic, peeled and minced

1/2 green bell pepper, seeded and chopped

1 large egg

1/2 teaspoon dried savory

1/2 teaspoon dried sage

sea salt and freshly ground black pepper to taste

1/2 pound pork sausage

1/2 pound ground sirloin

1/2 pound ground pork

1 1/2 cups crumbled cooked corn bread

1 (10-ounce) package frozen corn kernels, thawed

Preheat the oven to 350° F. Spray a 9 x 5 x 3–inch loaf pan with cooking spray.

Heat the oil in a large skillet, add the garlic, and sauté just until golden, which will take less than a minute. Add the chopped pepper and sauté briefly until bright green. Set aside to cool slightly.

In a large bowl, beat the egg and blend in the seasonings.

Add the ground meats and mix well. Add the sautéed garlic and pepper. Mix in the corn bread and corn kernels. Gently but firmly press the loaf ingredients into the prepared pan. Bake 45 minutes to 1 hour or until firm.

Sauces for Meat Loaf

We like to keep two of these sauces on hand at all times to serve with our meat loaf. Just remember that they are intended for people only—not for pets.

Fig Sauce

You're going to love this sauce!

2 to 3 tablespoons fresh lemon juice

1¹/₂ teaspoons cornstarch

1¹/₂ cups unsweetened grape juice

salt to taste

1 cup finely chopped dried figs

honey to taste

Combine the lemon juice and cornstarch in a saucepan and gradually stir in the grape juice. Add salt to your taste. Bring the mixture to a boil, stirring constantly, and simmer for about 6 minutes. Stir in the figs and cook about 2 to 3 minutes longer. Remove from the heat and add honey to your taste. This sauce must rest for 10 to 15 minutes to completely soften and amalgamate the figs.

Sorrel Sauce

This complex, slightly sour sauce is one of our favorites. It's delicious poured over turkey, veal, and chicken meat loaves!

MAKES 1½ CUPS

¾ cup chicken stock

1½ cups chopped fresh sorrel leaves

2 tablespoons butter

1½ tablespoons flour

½ cup heavy cream

juice of half a lemon

salt and white pepper to taste

Bring the stock to a boil, add the sorrel, and simmer 5 minutes. Pour into a blender or food processor and blend until very smooth.

Melt the butter in a saucepan over medium heat until it foams. Add the flour and stir briskly with a whisk. Cook a few minutes, stirring, to get rid of the raw flour taste but do not allow the mixture to brown.

Blend in the sorrel, then the cream and lemon juice, and season to taste with the salt and pepper.

Mushroom Sauce

We sometimes use sherry or good red wine instead of the lemon juice in this sauce. It will add delicious flavor to the simplest of meat loaves.

MAKES 2 CUPS

¹/₂ stick (4 tablespoons) unsalted butter

2 cloves garlic, peeled and finely minced

1 pound white mushrooms, trimmed and sliced (about 4 cups)

3 tablespoons all-purpose flour

1 large egg

1 cup half-and-half

1 tablespoon fresh lemon juice

¹/₄ teaspoon dried thyme

salt and white pepper to taste

nutmeg to taste

In a medium saucepan, heat 1 tablespoon of the butter, add the garlic, and sauté until the garlic is softened but not browned. Add the mushrooms and cook 2 minutes longer.

Remove the mushrooms from the pan and set them aside. Add the remaining butter to the pan and heat over medium heat until it foams. Add the flour and whisk constantly until completely combined. Cook about 5 minutes, stirring continually.

Beat the egg with the half-and-half in a small bowl and slowly stir into the butter mixture until it thickens. Slowly stir in the lemon juice, then the thyme, then the salt and pepper. Return the mushrooms to the sauce and heat, stirring constantly to blend the mushrooms with the liquid. Stir in the nutmeg.

Tomato Sauce

This is the easiest of all. Purchase a large jar of your favorite pasta or spaghetti sauce, pour it into a saucepan, add a little salt and pepper and maybe some wine, heat slowly, and pour it over your meat loaf. Two commercial sauces we're particularly fond of are:

Luna Rossa's Vodka Cream Pasta Sauce

Aunt Millie's All Natural Pasta Sauce

According to the American Pet Association, there are 68 million companion dogs in the U.S. today. Forty out of every 100 households own at least one dog, and in 2001 those dog-owning households spent almost 38 percent more dollars on pet paraphernalia than they did in 1996.

Why do people say they want a dog? According to the APA, a dog provides someone to play with, companionship, a way to help children learn, someone to communicate with, and security.

SIX

Raw and Offal Dinners for Dogs Only

Dogs thrive on some raw foods, and they love what the British politely call "variety meats," meaning such organs as the liver, kidneys, tongue, and heart of beasts and fowl. While dogs adore this kind of variety in their diet—we feed them a meal from this category at least once a week—we humans tend to think of them as "awful." So, do your dog a favor and serve him up a "dinner for one" from time to time—perhaps when you're dining out or having something like Spicy Orange Beef from the local Chinese restaurant.

Steak and Kidney Pie

If you have English relatives, they will fall all over this—especially if they're English setters. Our dogs report that the addition of puff pastry makes the pie really spectacular, although in the old country, plain piecrust made with lard was the traditional base.

MAKES ONE 9-INCH PIE

1 pound round steak, finely chopped

1 whole beef kidney (about 12 ounces) parboiled 10 minutes, drained, and sliced thin

¼ cup all-purpose flour

salt and freshly ground black pepper to taste

3 cloves garlic, peeled and chopped

1 tablespoon minced fresh parsley

1 cup beef broth

½ cup water

1 piece (about 8 ounces) frozen puff pastry, thawed

1 large egg, lightly beaten with 1 teaspoon water, for glaze

Preheat the oven to 425° F.

Place the steak and kidney in a bowl and toss with the flour and salt and pepper to taste. Add the garlic and parsley and toss again.

Transfer the mixture to a 9-inch deep-dish pie plate and pack it down.

In a bowl, stir together the broth and water, and pour it over the meat mixture until it comes halfway up the sides of the dish.

With a floured rolling pin, roll out the puff pastry on a lightly floured board to ⅛-inch thick and cut a strip long enough to fit all around the rim of the pie plate. Brush the lip of the dish with water, and press the strip of pastry onto it. Brush the strip with more water, and lay the rest of the pastry over the top to make a lid. Cut away any excess and crimp the edges shut.

Cut a ½-inch hole in the center to allow the steam to escape, and decorate the pie with any leftover pastry trimmings. (Our dogs were watching Jacques Pepin make these cute little sculptures on television one day and they turned to us and asked that we please make little sculptures of dogs chasing cats up a tree—done up in pastry. It seemed a small thing to ask. We aim to please.)

Chill the pie in the refrigerator for 10 minutes, then brush with the beaten egg and bake in the preheated oven until the pastry is golden and risen, about 20 minutes. Turn down the heat to 350° F, cover the pastry with foil, and continue cooking another 60 minutes, or until the meat is tender.

Calf's Liver with Bacon and Apples

Since dogs can't have onions, you'll have to make their favorite dish with bacon. But then, isn't everything better with bacon anyway? And apples keep the doctor away for Fido just as they do for you. Plus, you'll have this ready for the raving Rovers in less than half an hour.

MAKES 6 MEDIUM DOG SERVINGS

4 thick slices lean bacon

1/2 stick (4 tablespoons) unsalted butter

3 large Granny Smith apples, cored and sliced thin

2 tablespoons white wine vinegar

1 teaspoon sugar

1/4 cup dry white wine

1 1/2 pounds calf's liver, sliced 1/3-inch thick and cut into 2 x 1–inch strips

finely chopped fresh parsley leaves

In a large skillet, cook the bacon over moderate heat until crisp. Transfer it to paper towels to drain and pour off all but 2 tablespoons of the fat from the pan. To the fat remaining in the skillet, add 2 tablespoons of the butter and the apples, and cook over moderate heat, stirring occasionally, for about 10 minutes or until the apples are softened and light golden. Add the vinegar, sugar, and wine, bring the mixture to a boil, and boil for 3 minutes or until it is thickened. Transfer the mixture to a heated platter.

Wipe out the skillet, add the remaining 2 tablespoons of butter, and melt over high heat until the foam subsides. Pat the liver dry, add it to the butter, and cook, turning a few times, for 3 to 4 minutes or until it is browned on the outside and slightly pink within. Arrange the liver on top of the apple mixture, crumble the bacon over it, and sprinkle with the chopped parsley.

"Ever consider what they must think of us? I mean, here we come back from the grocery store with the most amazing haul—chicken, pork, half a cow. They must think we're the greatest hunters on earth!"
—Anne Tyler

Heart of My Heart Stew

Heart, kidney, tongue, and other offal choices are sold at ethnic grocers. Linda shops in a supermarket that caters to Latino and Eastern European customers, who snap up these items faster than you can say Jack Sprat. Our dogs lick the plate clean when we serve them this heart-y stew. Leftovers will keep for up to 6 months in the freezer. Just reheat to room temperature before serving.

MAKES 6 CUPS

1 veal or beef heart (about 1¹/₂ pounds)

kosher salt and freshly ground black pepper to taste

1 (5-ounce) can green peas, drained

¹/₂ cup dry barley

2 cups water

1 pan-cooked corn bread

Combine all the ingredients except the corn bread in a Crock-pot or stew pot. Simmer gently until the heart is tender, adding water as needed to maintain a soupy consistency. Can be left in the Crock-pot up to 8 hours. Remove the heart, cut it into bite-sized pieces, and return it to the stew. Serve warm with crumbled corn bread.

Judy's First Dog

Unlike Linda and Barbara, I grew up in an apartment in New York City. Dogs weren't exactly part of our family's lifestyle, but my father, a tough guy in many ways with a soft heart for animals, kept bringing them home.

One day he arrived with a cocker spaniel he said he'd bought from a guy on the street who was taking him to the pound. That dog went on to live a long and happy life with the bookkeeper in my father's office.

The next dog he brought home was a Dalmatian we named Kernel (not Colonel). The problem was that no one in the family was taking responsibility for walking him, and Kernel didn't seem to like walking much anyway. One of the few times I tried taking him out, he just lay down on the sidewalk and wouldn't budge, which was probably just as well because I wasn't allowed to cross streets alone.

So, in the end, Kernel went to live in my father's factory. It was in an industrial part of Brooklyn where you couldn't go out to the deli or even order in lunch, so there was a kitchen and a cook who provided meals for the small office staff and also for Kernel. One evening when my father was working late, he raided the refrigerator. The next day, an irate cook came out of the kitchen and demanded to know who had eaten the "nice beef stew" she'd made for the dog. My father assured her that it had, indeed, been very delicious.

So, I guess Kernel was my first dog, even though he didn't live at home very long. I didn't have another one until many years later. My first "grown-up" dog was Maxine, a Yorkshire terrier who died just a few months ago as I write this, one month short of her sixteenth birthday. Luckily, I still have Katie Scarlett, a red miniature poodle who turned two a few days ago. I still live in a New York apartment, and I will probably always have apartment-sized dogs.

Kidney and Kasha Stew

This is a weekly standard for our dogs. We try to make it when no company is expected in the house, because the aroma of stewing kidneys is attractive only to dogs. But boy, do they love it! And what could be simpler?

MAKES 6 CUPS

1 beef or pork kidney

1 cup kasha (buckwheat groats)

5 cloves garlic, peeled and smashed

1 tablespoon crumbled dried seaweed, sea kelp, or sea vegetable (see page 3)

6 cups water

Combine all the ingredients in a Crock-pot and simmer until tender. Chop the kidney, return it to the Crock-pot, and serve.

Raw Meaty Bones for Bowser

An entire movement has grown up around the notion of feeding dogs a raw diet. If you're interested, check out BARF (*www.barfworld.com*), the Web site, and read all about it. Although this sounds good in theory—after all, dogs evolved from wolves, who ate what they could catch—it seems to us a bit difficult to do in practice. And besides that, if our dogs ate only raw foods, we couldn't share their meals.

In fact, there is much controversy about feeding dogs bones either cooked or raw. Many veterinarians say never to give a dog bones—they have done surgery on dogs who have punctured their guts, and found shards of bone in their mouths.

At the other end of the spectrum are the BARF advocates, who believe that dogs should be fed nothing but raw foods and advocate giving them—for example—whole raw chickens, bones, skin, feet, head, and all.

In our experience, both these positions seem a bit extreme.

When we've asked people what they consider a raw diet, it seems to consist of nothing more than raw hamburger every day with a bone thrown in now and then. This seems to us as limited as a kibble diet. We believe in feeding our dogs a broad and varied diet of unprocessed foods—both raw and cooked—to give them the best chance for optimal health.

All that said, however, we know from experience that feeding the dogs raw, meaty knuckle and marrow beef bones has kept their teeth clean, their breath fresh, and their spirits uplifted as they spend many fruitful hours trying to decide where to hide those bones around the house for later pleasure. They always have one to work on, so we know they're getting the enzymes, amino acids, protein, calcium, fat, and trace minerals they couldn't get any other way.

And, yes, they sometimes leave one under the pillow just as a little love gift for us.

Here's a list of the raw, meaty bones we feed our dogs:

- Beef marrow and/or knuckle bones
- Beef neck bones
- Chicken and turkey necks (get the butcher to grind these for small dogs)

We usually buy our bones from a kosher butcher or at Whole Foods Market because that way we know we are getting the best-quality clean bones and meat.

We avoid any bone that might splinter or shard, including all bird bones, except those of the poor conventional chicken, who is kept for its short, miserable life in such confined quarters that it doesn't develop real bones. No turkey bones, no duck, no free-range chickens, no quail, dove, goose, or other bird that might actually have exercised and created strong bones. We also avoid pork bones, which tend to splinter, and any bones that are small enough for the dog to gulp down. Plain old big, hard beef bones with meat clinging to them seem best to us.

You will have to make your own decisions about giving bones to your dog. Especially if you have small dogs with little mouths, this may be problematic.

We do want to report, however, that one friend who has three small dogs, a shih tzu, a toy poodle, and a bichon frise, was spending a fortune on dog tooth-cleaning and fighting a losing battle with doggie bad breath until she began buying dog marrowbones and letting her little guys work on those. Now they're tartar-free and their breath is as sweet as a puppy's.

But, we must repeat, we are not veterinarians, nor do we claim any medical knowledge. We only know what works for us and our pets.

Raving Chicken Liver Rations

We serve this over brown rice. It's also a very good thing to serve over your dog's regular food during the period of transition to a natural diet.

MAKES ABOUT 4 CUPS

1 (10-ounce) package frozen peas and carrots (about 1½ cups)

1 cup chicken stock

¾ teaspoon poultry seasoning

1 pound chicken livers, rinsed and drained

2 tablespoons butter

sea salt to taste

Cook the peas and carrots according to package directions. Drain, return to the pan, and add the chicken stock and poultry seasoning. Heat gently.

Sauté the livers in the butter in a large skillet. When the livers are cooked through, about 10 minutes, add the peas and carrots, and stir to combine. Season with salt to taste.

Don't accept your dog's admiration as conclusive evidence that you are wonderful.—Ann Landers

The Wagging Tongues Have It

You may have to visit an ethnic grocer to find tongue for sale, but your dog will thank you. Those of us raised in cattle country can remember when our grandmothers all made pickled tongue. Today, we know it as a healthy, flavorful, low-calorie, high-fiber dish beloved by the not-so-beastly. This is a great Crock-pot no-fuss supper. Our dogs lick their bowls clean and pray for more whenever we cook it.

MAKES 8 CUPS

1 beef, pork, or lamb's tongue (about 1½ pounds total)

2 carrots, peeled and chopped

2 celery stalks with leaves, chopped

3 cups water

2 tablespoons mixed pickling spices

1 tablespoon crumbled dried seaweed, sea kelp, or sea vegetable (see page 3)

1 tablespoon red wine vinegar

salt and freshly ground black pepper to taste

1 tablespoon minced fresh parsley

2 cups cooked brown rice

Combine all the ingredients except the parsley and rice in a heavy stew pot or a Crock-pot and cook until the meat is tender, about 1 hour on the stovetop or up to 3 hours in the Crock-pot. Remove the tongue from the broth and chop fine. Taste the broth and adjust the seasoning with additional salt and pepper if necessary. Stir in the chopped tongue, parsley, and rice, and serve.

Gizzard Stew Made with Love

Revered in song and story, gizzard stew has an added advantage. It helps cure itchy skin. If you're suffering from hot spots, you might want to sip it yourself. Otherwise, feed it to the dog.

MAKES 8 CUPS

2 cups chicken gizzards

4 cloves garlic, peeled

1/2 teaspoon sage

1 cup barley

2 cups baby carrots

2 cups chopped beets

1 cup chopped beet tops

1 cup spinach

1 tablespoon crumbled dried seaweed, sea kelp, or sea vegetable (see page 3)

2 quarts water plus additional as needed

salt and freshly ground black pepper to taste

Combine all the ingredients in a stew pot or Crock-pot and simmer until the gizzards are fork tender, about 1 hour on the stove top or for up to 3 hours in a Crock-pot. Add more water as needed during cooking to maintain a soupy texture. When the stew is done, remove the gizzards and chop them, then return them to the pot. Taste and adjust seasoning with salt and pepper.

Steak Tartare

Dogs were onto this eat-raw-and-love-it idea long before we made it into a gourmet notion. As any dog will tell you, this dish relies on top-quality beef and the freshest eggs you can find. Serve with small rye crackers.

MAKES 6 CUPS

2 pounds best-quality ground sirloin

2 tablespoons capers, plus additional for garnish

2 tablespoons olive oil

salt to taste

6 anchovy fillets, cut in small pieces, plus additional for garnish

Worcestershire sauce to taste

dash of Tabasco

generous grinding of black pepper

1 tablespoon red wine vinegar

2 large egg yolks

1/4 cup chopped parsley

1/2 teaspoon Dijon mustard

In a large bowl, combine all the ingredients and mix carefully with a fork to retain the fluffy texture. Gently shape the mixture into a loaf and garnish it with additional anchovy strips and capers. Cover and chill for 20 minutes or so before serving.

SEVEN

From the Barkery—
Just Desserts

Want a good excuse to make dessert? *I'm doing this for my dog!* You and your pooch will thank each other for these healthy sweet treats from the barkery. And always remember, the most universally acknowledged "no-no" food for dogs is chocolate, which causes a form of tachycardia (racing heart) that has killed many a canine. Don't leave chocolate **in any form** lying around where your dog can get it. Our friend Jennifer English, host of the Food and Wine Radio Network, had a close call when a vendor sent her a box of extremely fancy chocolates (the purer the chocolate, the more lethal it is) and her pug, Beauregard, got into them. Luckily, Beau's life was saved by an alert vet, but Jennifer learned her lesson the hard way.

Bowser's Birthday Pawty Cake

We love to make this cake in the shape of a dog bone by using a 9-inch square pan and four 9-inch round pans to form the bone. For the "platter," cover a thick piece of 12 x 18–inch cardboard with birthday party wrap or foil. If you don't want to get that fancy, however, you can simply make a three-layer cake using three 10-inch round pans. Both people and their pets will love it, whatever shape you choose, and it's good for you besides.

CAKE:

3 cups whole-wheat flour

1 tablespoon baking soda

1/2 teaspoon salt

1 1/2 cups smooth peanut butter

3 large eggs

3/4 cup olive oil

1 tablespoon pure vanilla extract

1 cup honey

3 cups grated carrots

1 cup raisins

FROSTING:

16 ounces cream cheese

2 sticks (1/2 pound) unsalted butter

6 cups confectioners' sugar

1 1/2 tablespoons milk

2 teaspoons pure vanilla extract

Preheat the oven to 400° F. Spray four 9-inch round and one 9-inch square pan with Pam for Baking or Baker's Joy.

In the bowl of an electric mixer, stir together the flour, baking soda, and salt. Add the peanut butter, eggs, oil, vanilla, and honey. Beat on high for 2 minutes. Fold in the carrots and raisins. Divide evenly among the prepared pans and bake 15 minutes or until a toothpick inserted in the middle comes out clean.

Cool in the pans 3 minutes, then turn onto a rack to cool completely.

To make the frosting, beat the cream cheese and butter until fluffy, then add the sugar, milk, and vanilla and beat to a spreadable consistency.

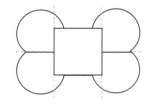

To form the dog bone, cut about 1/6 off the top and one side of each of the 4 round cakes. Set the square cake in the center of the prepared cardboard base. Add two round cakes at each end, abutting the cut edges to each other.

Frost the cake and write "Happy Birthday, Bowser" with colored frosting from a can if you wish. Or, sprinkle dried banana or other dried fruits on the top.

The cake can be made a day or so ahead and stored in the refrigerator until serving. The carrots will keep it moist (always a big consideration for discriminating dogs who hate dry cake).

Party Pup Cakes with Apple and Cheddar

Even if you forgot Baby's birthday until the last minute, you'll be able to celebrate because these pup cakes take almost no time at all.

MAKES 18 PUP CAKES

CAKES:

1¹/₂ cups white whole-wheat flour (see note, page 74)

¹/₄ cup oatmeal

2 teaspoons baking powder

¹/₂ teaspoon baking soda

¹/₂ cup plain yogurt

¹/₂ cup water

¹/₄ cup vegetable oil

2 tablespoons honey

2 large eggs

1 large apple, cored and minced

1 cup grated Cheddar cheese

FROSTING:

8 ounces Neufchatel or cream cheese

2 tablespoons honey

2 tablespoons plain yogurt

2 to 3 tablespoons whole-wheat flour

chopped walnuts, for garnish

grated carrots, for garnish

Preheat the oven to 400° F. Spray 18 paper-lined muffin cups with Baker's Joy or Pam for Baking.

In a large bowl, combine the flour, oatmeal, baking powder, and baking soda.

In a medium bowl, blend together the yogurt, water, oil, honey, and eggs, then stir in the apple and cheese. Add to the flour mixture and stir just until barely mixed.

Spoon the batter into the muffin tins, filling each cup about three-quarters full. Bake in the preheated oven about 20 minutes or until a toothpick inserted into the center of a pup cake comes out clean. Let the pup cake cool in the tins on a rack for a few minutes, then remove and set them aside to cool completely.

For the frosting, combine the Neufchatel or cream cheese, honey, and yogurt until smooth. Add just enough flour to thicken the frosting to a good spreading consistency. Frost the cooled pup cakes, sprinkle them with chopped walnuts, and top with grated carrots. Grrrrreat!

Tarte Tatin

An apple a day keeps the veterinarian away, but I'll bet those French sisters who invented this classic tart had no idea how popular their famous dessert would be with dogs. Served with unsweetened whipped cream, even our cats eat it. And, made with puff pastry, it's a snap. We know that when you buy a tarte Tatin from a patisserie, the apple slices are fanned out just so, but hey, this one's for you and your dogs. Simply slice the apples thin and arrange them any which way. The flavor's just as good.

MAKES 6 SERVINGS

½ **stick (¼ cup) unsalted butter**

½ **cup dark brown sugar**

8 or so unpeeled Gala or Granny Smith apples, cored and sliced thin

1 sheet frozen puff pastry (from a 17¼-ounce package), thawed

½ **cup whipping cream**

Preheat the oven to 400° F.

Place the butter in a 10-inch cast-iron (or other ovenproof) skillet and melt it over medium-low heat. Add the brown sugar and stir to melt. As you core and cut the apples, toss the slices into the sizzling butter mixture. Cook the apples until tender over medium heat, about 5 to 8 minutes. Turn off the heat and let the apples cool in the pan.

While the apples are cooling, roll out the pastry on a lightly floured surface with a floured rolling pin to about 11 inches square. Drape the pastry over the apples in the skillet, tucking the edges under.

Bake the tart in the preheated oven about 15 minutes or until golden brown. Cool 15 minutes.

While the tart cools, beat the cream to soft peaks. Just before serving, place a platter with a lip over the skillet and, using two potholders, hold the skillet and plate tightly together and flip the tart over onto the plate. Cut into wedges and serve warm.

Bowser's Blondies with Pumpkin

Healthy, delicious, and easy to make, these puppy treats will be hard to resist—for you, we mean. Chewy, sweet, and made with white whole-wheat flour that delivers a nutritional punch (see page 74), they're something of a miracle.

MAKES ABOUT 3 DOZEN BARS

2¼ cups white whole-wheat flour

2½ teaspoons baking powder

2 teaspoons ground cinnamon

¼ teaspoon salt

1½ cups packed brown sugar

¾ cup (1½ sticks) butter, softened

1 teaspoon pure vanilla extract

2 large eggs

1 cup pumpkin puree

Preheat the oven to 350° F. Grease a 15 x 10–inch jellyroll pan.

Combine the flour, baking powder, cinnamon, and salt in a medium bowl.

Beat the sugar, butter, and vanilla extract together in another bowl with an electric mixer. Add the eggs one at a time, beating well after each addition. Then beat in the pumpkin. Gradually beat in the flour mixture into the egg mixture.

Spread the batter in the prepared pan and bake in the preheated oven 20 to 25 minutes or until a wooden toothpick inserted in the center comes out clean. Cool completely in the pan, then cut into 2 x 4–inch bars. Store airtight in a tin.

Profiteroles

You're not the only one who will love these small cream puffs. Your pooch will love them, too. They are a bit time-consuming, however, so you and your pal will probably need a nice long nap once you're done.

MAKES 48 SMALL PUFFS

PUFFS:

1 cup water

1/2 cup (1 stick) unsalted butter, cut into pieces

1 cup white whole-wheat flour (see page 74)

1/4 teaspoon salt

4 large eggs

PASTRY CREAM:

1 tablespoon water

1/2 teaspoon unflavored gelatin

2 cups whole milk

2/3 cup whipping cream

1 teaspoon pure vanilla extract

6 large egg yolks

2 tablespoons mild honey

1/2 cup white whole-wheat flour

pinch of salt

confectioners' sugar for sprinkling the puffs

To make the puffs, bring the water and butter to a boil in a heavy medium saucepan. Reduce the heat to low and stir in the flour and salt. Stir constantly until the mixture is smooth and pulls away from the sides of the pan, forming a ball, about 1 minute. Transfer the dough ball to a large bowl and beat in the eggs, one at a time, blending well after each addition. Cover the dough loosely with plastic wrap and set it aside to cool for about 1 hour.

Preheat the oven to 425° F. Line 2 large baking sheets with lightly buttered parchment paper or cover the sheets with silicone-impregnated mats (Silpats). Spoon the dough into a pastry bag fitted with a 1/2-inch plain tip. Pipe 1-inch rounds onto the prepared baking sheets, spacing them about 1 inch apart. Or, alternatively, use two spoons to pinch off bits of dough about the size of bubble-gum balls and drop them onto the pan. Whichever method you choose, moisten your fingertips and smooth the rounds.

Bake in the preheated oven until golden brown and puffed, about 23 to 25 minutes.

Remove the puffs from the oven and turn off the heat. Pierce one side of each puff with the tip of a small knife or a skewer. Return the puffs to the turned-off oven and let them stand with the door ajar for a few minutes. Remove them from the oven and cool completely.

To make the pastry cream, put the water into a small bowl and sprinkle the gelatin over it.

Bring the milk, cream, and vanilla to a simmer in a large, heavy saucepan.

In a large bowl, whisk together the egg yolks, honey, flour, and salt. Gradually whisk in the hot milk mixture, then pour this new mixture into the saucepan. Whisk over medium heat until the cream thickens and boils, about 1 minute. Stir in the gelatin mixture. Transfer the filling to a medium bowl. Press plastic wrap directly onto the surface and chill. The cream can be made a day in advance and refrigerated until you're ready to use it.

Spoon the pastry cream into a pastry bag fitted with a ¼-inch plain tip. Insert the tip into the cut on each puff and fill the puffs with cream. Alternately, spoon the cream into the puffs with a small teaspoon. Serve at once or cover and refrigerate for up to 48 hours. Sprinkle with confectioners' sugar just before serving.

I think animal testing is a terrible idea: They get all nervous and give the wrong answers.—Anonymous

Carob Éclairs

These are really profiteroles shaped like dog bones, filled with pastry cream, and iced with a glorious glaze. We know dogs can't eat chocolate, but they seem to thrive on carob, which comes from the leguminous pods of the locust tree, a tree that is indigenous to the Mediterranean. Carob powder, a healthier alternative to cocoa powder, is made from roasted and ground carob pods. It is a very rich source of calcium and potassium, and unlike cocoa it is naturally sweet and contains no caffeine or oxalic acid. You can find it in most health food stores.

MAKES 24 SMALL ÉCLAIRS

1 cup water

1/4 teaspoon kosher salt

8 tablespoons (1 stick) unsalted butter, cut into small pieces

1 cup white whole-wheat flour (see page 74)

4 large eggs

1 recipe pastry cream (see page 108)

1 recipe Carob Ganache (recipe follows)

Preheat the oven to 350° F. Line two baking sheets with lightly buttered parchment paper or cover them with silicone-impregnated mats (Silpats).

Combine the water, salt, and butter in a heavy saucepan and bring to a boil. Add the flour all at once and stir vigorously until the mixture pulls away from the sides of the pan, about 5 minutes. Add 3 of the eggs, one at a time, beating continuously until the mixture is smooth and shiny. Chill the dough in the refrigerator for 30 minutes or so.

Fill a pastry bag fitted with a #7 plain round tip with the chilled dough and pipe it out into 3- to 4-inch lengths about ½-inch high on the prepared baking sheets. Beat the remaining egg and brush the éclairs with the egg.

Bake in the preheated oven for 20 minutes, then reduce the heat to 325° F and continue baking another 7 minutes, or until the éclairs are golden brown all over. Remove them from the oven and set them aside to cool. Make a small slit in one side of each éclair with a knife or a skewer. Spoon the pastry cream into a pastry bag fitted with a plain round tip and pipe it into the slits, or spoon it in with a tiny spoon. Using an offset spatula, glaze the tops with the Carob Ganache.

The éclairs can be stored, covered, in the refrigerator for up to 48 hours.

Carob Ganache

Chocolate revs up a dog's heart and can kill your best pal (think doggie crack cocaine), so always substitute healthy carob in any recipe calling for chocolate or cocoa.

MAKES 1½ CUPS

¾ **cup heavy cream**

1 (8 ounce) carob bar, chopped

Bring the cream to a boil in a heavy saucepan over medium heat. Turn off the heat, add the chopped carob, and let the mixture stand until the carob is almost melted. Stir with a rubber spatula to finish melting and mix thoroughly. Pour the ganache into a bowl, cover it with plastic wrap, and refrigerate it about 45 minutes until firm.

Coco Loco Bites

Once you've toasted the oats, these healthy, yummy cookies don't require any further baking. Simply roll 'em up and put 'em in a tin until ready to serve. Shaped like frosted doggie bones, they are bound to please. No need to mention to the pooch that they're also chock-full of calcium, complex carbohydrates, and trace minerals.

MAKES ABOUT 40 COOKIES

1½ cups old-fashioned rolled oats

1 cup smooth peanut butter

1½ cups nonfat dry milk

4 tablespoons (½ stick) unsalted butter

2 tablespoons honey

½ cup carob chips

½ cup flaked coconut

Preheat the oven to 350° F.

Spread the oats on an ungreased baking pan and toast them in the preheated oven, stirring occasionally, until lightly browned, about 10 minutes. Set them aside to cool.

In a medium bowl, combine the peanut butter and nonfat dry milk. Stir in the toasted oats and set aside.

Melt the butter in a small saucepan over medium heat. Stir in the honey and pour the butter mixture over the oats. Stir until well combined, and set aside to cool slightly.

Shape the mixture into about 40 dog-bone logs, each about 2½ inches long. Place the logs on a wire rack or a parchment-lined baking sheet and set them aside.

Place the carob chips in a glass measuring cup and microwave on high for 45 seconds to 1 minute, or melt on the stovetop in a double boiler. Stir until the chips are completely melted. Dip each cookie about halfway into the melted carob or drizzle them with the melted carob. Sprinkle the cookies with the coconut and let them stand until the carob is set. Store, tightly covered, in the refrigerator.

Counter Surfer's Cookies

If your dog is tall enough to reach the countertop, you'll have to keep these in a cupboard, out of his reach. On the other hand, they're full of antioxidants, vitamins C, E, and B, zinc, and valuable fiber, so even if he manages to sneak a few behind your back, they won't hurt him—and they're not bad for you either.

MAKES 20 LARGE COOKIES

1 cup unsweetened crushed pineapple, drained, juice reserved

1/4 cup olive oil

1/4 cup honey

1 large egg

1 teaspoon pure vanilla extract

2 cups white whole-wheat flour (see page 74)

1 1/2 teaspoons baking powder

1/4 teaspoon baking soda

1/2 cup chopped walnuts

Preheat the oven to 350° F. Line a baking sheet with well-greased parchment paper or a silicone-impregnated mat (Silpat).

In a large mixing bowl whisk together the pineapple, oil, honey, egg, and vanilla. Add the flour, baking powder, baking soda, and walnuts and stir well to combine, adding some of the reserved pineapple juice as needed to form a soft dough.

Drop the dough by the tablespoonful onto the prepared baking sheet about 1/2 inch apart, and bake in the preheated oven for 20 minutes or until golden brown. Cool on a rack. Store in an airtight tin.

Banana Mutt Bread

In case you were wondering what to do with those two nearly black bananas on the kitchen counter, we've got the answer. Make bread for the dog—and yourself. Note that this bread is not all sugared up. Better for your health and Bowser's as well.

MAKES 1 LOAF

2¹/2 cups unsifted whole-wheat flour

3¹/2 teaspoons baking powder

1 teaspoon salt

¹/4 cup honey

1 large egg

3 tablespoons olive oil

³/4 cup whole milk

1 cup mashed ripe bananas

¹/2 cup chopped walnuts

Preheat the oven to 325° F. Spray a 9 x 5 x 3–inch loaf pan with Pam for Baking or Baker's Joy.

Place all the dry ingredients in a large bowl and whisk to combine. Make a well in the center and add the honey, egg, oil, and milk. Stir to combine with the flour mixture. Add the bananas and nuts and mix just until incorporated.

Pour the batter into the prepared loaf pan and bake in the preheated oven 55 to 60 minutes. The bread is done when a sharp knife inserted in the center comes out clean.

Cool in the pan on a rack for 2 to 3 minutes, then remove from the pan and cool another 15 minutes.

Note: You can use the same batter to make banana-nut muffins. This quantity will make 6 to 8 muffins.

Fleas Navidad Nuthins

So, you're having a Christmas Eve party. Want to include the pooches? Whip up these festive muffins. Just try keeping the two-legged beasts out of them. Double dog dare you.

MAKES 48 REGULAR OR 96 MINI-MUFFINS

2 tablespoons honey

2¼ cups warm water

¼ cup applesauce

1 teaspoon pure vanilla extract

2 large eggs

4 cups whole-wheat flour

1 teaspoon salt

1 tablespoon baking powder

1 tablespoon ground cinnamon

½ teaspoon Aleppo or cayenne pepper

1 cup chopped pecans

½ cup craisins or golden raisins

Preheat the oven to 400° F. Line regular or mini-muffin cups with paper liners.

In the bowl of an electric mixer, combine the honey, water, applesauce, vanilla, and eggs and mix until foamy. Add the flour, salt, baking powder, cinnamon, and pepper. Mix until smooth. Fold in the pecans and craisins.

Place a heaping tablespoon of the batter in each regular muffin tin, OR a heaping teaspoon in each mini-muffin tin. Bake until golden brown, about 15 minutes for regular and 10 minutes for minis. Cool on a rack and store in an airtight tin.

Frosty Paws

This is an outdoor treat unless you're prepared to mop up after the slobbery mutts.

32 ounces plain or vanilla yogurt

1 ripe banana

2 tablespoons smooth all-natural peanut butter (with no added sugar or salt)

2 tablespoons honey

Combine all ingredients in a food processor and puree. Transfer to Dixie cups (we like toothbrushing size). Fill ¾ full, then place the cups on a baking sheet and transfer to the freezer. Once the paws are frozen, place them in zip-lock bags. To serve, pop the "paws" out of the cups—in the backyard, please—and stand back while your canine connoisseurs enjoy this postprandial thrill.

VARIATION: Spring Tonic Frosty Paws

1 cup wheat grass

½ cup cottage cheese of your choice

2 cups low-sodium chicken or vegetable broth

Puree the wheat grass and cottage cheese in a food processor, then add the broth and mix. Proceed as for regular Frosty Paws above.

EIGHT

Give the Poor Dog a Bone (and Other Treats)

Many of these treats will be as tasty for your friends as they are for Fido, but some—like the liver treats—may require a specialized palate.

We don't recommend spoiling anyone, man or beast, with too many treats, but these are all healthy, and those made with liver are a good way to add an important nutrient to your best pal's diet.

Westminster Dog Show Chicken Liver Treats

Ever wonder how they get all those dogs to perform so flawlessly? Small bites of these liver treats usually do the trick. We know one trainer who holds a few on the inside of his cheek during a show, so that he can surreptitiously pull one out of his mouth and pop it into the dog's. Under normal circumstances, however, it won't be necessary for you to "pre-taste" these treats. Just keep them in an airtight tin and watch your dog sit up and beg for more.

MAKES 24 SMALL TREATS

1 pound chicken livers

2 large eggs

2 tablespoons molasses

1¹/₂ cups cornmeal

¹/₂ teaspoon garlic powder

Preheat the oven to 400° F. Grease a 9 x 9–inch baking pan.

Puree the liver, eggs, and molasses in a food processor. Add the remaining ingredients and blend well.

Pour the mixture into the prepared pan and bake in the preheated oven 25 to 30 minutes or until dark brown and shiny. Cool and cut or break into bite-sized pieces. Store in an airtight tin in the refrigerator.

50 Ways for Your Dog to Love Her Liver (Treats)

Groomers love them. Trainers swear by them. Dogs can't get enough of these liver treats. They're quite different from the previous recipe, which is made with chicken livers. These produce a drier, more cracker-like product.

MAKES ABOUT 50 TREATS

2 tablespoons extra-virgin olive oil

1 pound beef or pork liver

1 cup white whole-wheat flour (see page 74)

1/2 cup stone-ground cornmeal

2 tablespoons dried garlic flakes

2 tablespoons dried parsley flakes

Preheat the oven to 350° F. Coat a 10 x 16–inch baking sheet with oil.

Combine all the ingredients in a food processor and process to make a rough puree.

Oil your hands well and press the mixture into a big, flat patty. Score the cake into 2 x 2–inch squares. Bake in the preheated oven for 20 minutes or until brown. Cool on a rack, and then break up into treat-sized pieces. Refrigerate tightly covered for up to 3 weeks, or freeze for up to 6 months.

Tuna Terrific Treats

Adding brewer's yeast to dog and cat food provides fatty acids and B-complex vitamins. It also helps deter fleas. Both dogs and cats will love these fishy finds.

MAKES 18 TREATS

1 (6-ounce) can Italian chunk tuna in oil, drained, and crumbled (oil reserved)

1 cup Italian-style bread crumbs

1 tablespoon oil reserved from the tuna can

1 large egg

Preheat the oven to 350° F. Spray a 9 x 9-inch pan with nonstick cooking spray.

Combine all the ingredients in a bowl and mix thoroughly. Pat the dough evenly onto the prepared pan and score it into 1 x 2–inch pieces. Bake in the preheated oven for 10 minutes or until golden.

Cool on a rack, then break into pieces and refrigerate tightly covered for up to 3 weeks, or freeze for up to 6 months.

If you think dogs can't count, try putting three dog biscuits in your pocket and then giving Fido only two of them.—Phil Pastoret

Peanut Butter Buddy Bones

Dogs pig out on these crisp, nutty treats. Take care that you don't do likewise. Great reward cookies. Sit. Stay. Roll over. Not you! The dog!

MAKES ABOUT 100 DIAMOND-SHAPED OR 50 BONE-SHAPED CRACKERS

3 cups white whole-wheat flour (see page 74)

1/2 cup stone-ground cornmeal

1/8 cup powdered milk

1/2 teaspoon salt

1 tablespoon baking powder

2 tablespoons honey

1 cup smooth peanut butter

1 1/4 cups water, or enough to make stiff dough

Preheat the oven to 400° F.

Combine all the ingredients in a food processor and process to make a stiff dough, adding more water if needed. The dough should be stiff enough to form a ball that rides around the blade.

Divide the dough in half. Roll each piece on a lightly floured surface to a 1/4-inch-thick 12-inch square. Cut into diamonds or dog bone shapes with a cookie cutter.*

Transfer the treats to an ungreased baking sheet and bake in the preheated oven for 10 minutes. Turn off the heat and cool in the oven with the door ajar. These will keep for up to 3 weeks in an airtight tin.

*Note: Bone-shaped cookie cutters are available in bakeware and pet supply stores.

Brodie's Ranch Biscuits

These crunchy, dark biscuits are named in honor of Barbara's sweet dog Brodie, who was the first to wolf them down. All her dogs have been loving them ever since. Try them and you'll see why. The biscuits make very nice gifts for friends' pets. If you want to get really fancy, you can cut them into dog-bone shapes and tie them to a wreath with ribbon for a super-duper doggie Christmas gift. For everyday use, we usually just roll them out and cut them into biscuit shapes or diamonds.

MAKES 30 SMALL, 25 MEDIUM, OR 15 LARGE DOG BONES

2 eggs

1 pound 90-percent-lean ground beef

3 cups white whole-wheat flour, plus additional as needed (see page 74)

1 cup rolled oats

1 cup chicken broth

2 teaspoons fresh garlic, peeled and chopped

1 teaspoon crumbled dried seaweed, sea kelp, or sea vegetable (see page 3)

Preheat oven to 350° F. Grease two baking sheets.

Combine the eggs and ground beef in a food processor and blend well.

Combine the flour and rolled oats in a large mixing bowl. Add the ground-beef mixture and mix with your hands until well blended.

Add the garlic and seaweed to the chicken broth and stir all but 2 tablespoons into the beef mixture. The dough will be sticky. Divide it into 2 balls.

Knead each dough ball on a well-floured surface for 2 to 3 minutes, adding small amounts of flour until the dough is no longer sticky.

Roll each piece into a ½-inch-thick round on a well-floured surface. Cut the dough into the shapes and sizes you prefer.

Before baking, brush the biscuits with the remaining 2 tablespoons of chicken-broth mixture. Arrange the biscuits on the prepared baking sheets, and bake in the preheated oven for 45 minutes to 1 hour. Do not overbake. Cool to room temperature on a rack and store in a container with a loose-fitting lid, such as a cookie jar.

Poochie Pill Poppers

Let's face it, at some time in your pet's life, medications will be necessary, and this recipe is the answer to getting the reluctant pooch to take his pills. Form the dough into balls and punch holes partway through with a screwdriver. Just remember to make the holes large enough so that you'll have room to insert the pills after baking. We guarantee that your dog will never again resist popping a pill. But if you're not using these as medicine balls, you can cut them into various shapes with a cookie cutter. We like to give them as hostess gifts to animal lovers.

MAKES ABOUT 60 MEDIUM-SIZED BISCUITS

3 cups whole-wheat flour

2 teaspoons garlic powder

1 large egg, beaten

1 cup buttermilk

1 cup shredded Cheddar cheese

½ cup extra-virgin olive oil

Preheat the oven to 400° F. Lightly grease a large baking sheet.

Combine the flour and garlic powder in a large mixing bowl. Make a well in the center and gradually stir in the egg, buttermilk, cheese, and oil until well blended.

Knead the dough on a floured surface for 3 to 4 minutes. Roll out to ¼-inch thick. Cut using your favorite cutter and/or roll into the appropriate size treats for your pets.

Arrange the biscuits on the prepared baking sheet, and bake in the preheated oven about 25 minutes or until golden.

Cool on a rack and store at room temperature for 2 to 3 weeks in a container with a loose-fitting lid.

Note: After baking, we sometimes brush these cookies with honey mixed with a little bit of chicken broth. Dogs love the taste.

Collie Flour Biscuits

Toss these to the dogs while they're still warm and you'll have devoted doggies for the rest of the day. If you can only find regular whole-wheat flour, no one will whine or tuck his tail between his legs over the substitution.

MAKES 8 TO 10 BISCUITS

2 cups white whole-wheat flour (see page 74)

1¹/₂ teaspoons baking powder

¹/₂ teaspoon kosher or sea salt

³/₈ cup unsalted butter

³/₈ cup buttermilk

Preheat the oven to 425° F. Grease a medium baking sheet.

Sift the flour, baking powder, and salt into a bowl. Cut in the butter with two knives until the mixture resembles coarse crumbs. Add the buttermilk, mixing lightly with a fork just until the dough holds together.

Transfer the dough to a lightly floured surface and knead lightly. Roll it out to ½-inch thick. Cut into rounds or other shapes with a floured cookie cutter.

Transfer the biscuits to the prepared baking sheet and bake in the preheated oven for 12 to 15 minutes.

Note: The dogs like these brushed with raw organic honey, while we prefer ours with a pat of butter. Very tasty indeed!

Rice-a-Romper Garlic Parsley Muffins

If your pooch has a tummyache, a nice serving of rice will set it right. And besides that, using up that container of white rice you got with your Chinese take-out the other day will undoubtedly make you feel better, too.

MAKES 12 MUFFINS

1 cup cooked rice (white or brown)

1 cup skim milk

2 tablespoons extra-virgin olive oil

1 cup all-purpose white flour

1 tablespoon baking powder

1/4 teaspoon kosher salt

3 cloves garlic, peeled and minced

2 tablespoons minced fresh parsley

3 large egg whites, beaten to stiff peaks

Preheat the oven to 350° F. Line 12 muffin cups with paper liners and spray them with nonstick cooking spray.

Combine the rice, milk, and oil in a large bowl and mix well. Stir in the flour, baking powder, salt, garlic, and parsley. Fold in the beaten egg whites. Fill muffin tins ¾ full and bake in the preheated oven for 25 minutes or until golden brown. Cool on a rack and store in a tin with a tight-fitting lid.

Hot Dog Bites

These hot dog bites are definitely for both you and the dogs.

MAKES 2 (PEOPLE) SERVINGS

1 teaspoon olive oil

¼ teaspoon garlic powder

3 organic turkey franks cut into bite-sized pieces

Combine the oil and garlic powder and brush over the franks. Broil, turning until evenly browned.

Insert toothpicks for the people and serve warm. Do not give the dogs toothpicks.

Hush Puppies

Nothing simpler, nothing more satisfying. All your puppies will hush because they're so busy eating.

MAKES 1 DOZEN

1 cup white cornmeal

1/2 cup whole milk

1/4 teaspoon kosher salt

2 tablespoons vegetable oil

1 egg, well beaten

2 slices bacon, cooked and crumbled (optional)

Preheat oven to 400° F. Grease a medium baking sheet.

Stir together all the ingredients, including the bacon if using it. Drop the batter by the spoonful onto the prepared baking sheet and bake in the preheated oven for 15 minutes or until golden brown.

Barking Biscotti

This makes golden, crunchy, nutty-flavored biscotti. Dip yours in your coffee. The dog kids prefer theirs as is.

MAKES 40 MINI-BISCUITS

1/2 **cup all-purpose flour**

2 **cups whole-wheat flour**

1/4 **cup stone-ground cornmeal**

1/2 **cup shelled sunflower seeds**

3 **large eggs**

1/4 **cup buttermilk**

2 **tablespoons unsalted butter, softened**

1/4 **cup molasses**

Preheat the oven to 350° F.

In a large bowl, combine the flours, cornmeal, and sunflower seeds.

In a small bowl, whisk the eggs and buttermilk together. Reserve 1 to 2 tablespoons of the egg mixture in a separate dish for glazing the biscotti.

Make a well in the center of the flour mixture and gradually stir in the softened butter, molasses, and egg mixture until well blended.

Divide the dough into 2 balls and knead each ball on a floured surface for 2 to 3 minutes or until it's no longer sticky. Roll the dough out to 1/4 to 1/2 inch thick. Cut with a canine-themed or mini-biscuit cutter and place the biscotti on an ungreased baking sheet. Brush the reserved egg mixture over the tops of the biscotti.

Bake in the preheated oven about 30 minutes or until golden.

Turn off the heat and let the biscotti cool for several hours in the oven with the door closed.

Store at room temperature in a container with a loose-fitting lid.

Dog Gone Flea Biscuits

We are opposed to flea collars because many pets are allergic to them and they can cause eye problems as well as breathing problems—not to mention hot spots. Yeast is a natural flea repellent. This is a nice little remedy for your flea-bitten pets. Store the biscuits in an airtight tin.

MAKES 90 TO 100 BISCUITS

½ cup whole-wheat flour

1½ cups all-purpose flour

1 cup rye flour

1 cup quick-cooking rolled oats

1 cup stone-ground cornmeal

¼ cup brewer's yeast

2 tablespoons garlic powder

½ cup olive oil

1 large egg, beaten

1 cup chicken broth

Preheat the oven to 300° F. Line a baking sheet with foil.

In a large mixing bowl, combine all the dry ingredients.

Make a well in the center and gradually stir in the oil, egg, and chicken broth until well blended.

Divide the dough into 2 balls and knead each one on a floured surface for 3 to 5 minutes. Roll out each piece of dough to between ¼ and ½ inch thick.

Cut the dough with a dog-bone or other cutter and place the shapes on the prepared baking sheet.

Bake in the preheated oven for 30 minutes. Cool the biscuits on a rack until firm, and store at room temperature in an airtight tin, or freeze them for up to a year.

NINE

Pooch Parties

Want to put a smile on your dog's face? Give her a nice party. Whether it's her birthday, Howl-a-Ween, or even Christmas, don't leave your best friend out of the festivities. If you'd like to raise money for your local dog rescue or shelter, why not have a dog cotillion? Dogs are such good dancers. Up on their hind legs, all smiles and pants, they do love to boogie down.

Planning a party for a pup requires more than just food. Once you have determined the theme, you will need party hats, bandanas, games, and party favors. For appropriate toys and games, see *www.thedoggiestore.com/dogtoys.html*.

You'll also need to find the perfect party site. We prefer fenced outdoor venues for our celebrations. That way, we can simply hose down the grounds—and perhaps the guests—once the party is done and everybody is caked in cake from stem to stern.

Send out personalized e-vites by logging on to *www.petpages.com* and clicking on Pet Greetings. They have a number of cool cards complete with howling good music.

Bowser's Birthday Party:
A Six-Course Celebration

Our dogs are really into Italian food these days, so we planned this birthday party to celebrate the best of the boot. Opera plays in the background. If our guests are so moved, they may howl with the arias. Others, less musically inclined, want the games to start.

But first, all guests are given a favor—a bandana color-coordinated to our birthday girl's. Check out *www.bandanaswholesale.com* to find the pawfect bandana for your party. And, of course, there are party hats. See *www.alexis-creations.com* for the very latest in doggie frocks and hats. Pass out throwaway cameras for the two-legged guests to record the festivities and you're ready to go.

Passed hors d'oeuvres include Peanut Butter Buddy Bones, Chicken "Brownies," and Turkey Polenta Pups. Even the main course, Spaghetti Squares with Fresh Mozzarella and Tomato, can be eaten out of hand or paw.

Just be sure there's plenty of food to go around so there's no snarling or grabbing. Offer lots of water to slurp up and remember to sing happy birthday when the cake is brought out.

THE MENU

Peanut Butter Buddy Bones (page 121)

Chicken "Brownies" (page 29)

Turkey Polenta Pups (page 30)

Spaghetti Squares with Mozzarella and Tomato (page 60)

Party Pup Cakes with Apple and Cheddar (page 105)

Bowser's Birthday Pawty Cake (page 104)

Frosty Paws (page 116)

A Happy Canine Christmas

It's about the joy of sharing and giving, so you'll want to encourage your dogs to share at the party. Yeah, right! Just make sure you supply plenty of treats and Santa hats for all, and your party will be a smash. Make goodie bags of the Fleas Navidad Nuthins. What could be better than an all-natural dog biscuit that helps repel fleas? Now that's a thoughtful gift, don't you think? And you can make them a few days ahead.

The Turkey Loaf can be baked in advance and frozen, and the salad can be prepared the night before. That leaves only the éclairs to make on the day of the party.

THE MENU

Fleas Navidad Nuthins (page 115)

Carrot Craisin Salad (page 47)

Ms. B's Holiday Turkey Loaf (page 80)

Carob Éclairs (page 110)

Howl-a-Ween

If ever there was a party opportunity that appeals to dogs, it's Howl-a-Ween. Dogs love to dress up, and there are all kinds of costumes available online and in pet shops everywhere.

Maybe a few of your guests will know some tricks, but even if they don't, fill their treat bags in advance with Coco Loco Bites.

Since it's their party, let them bob for tennis balls instead of apples and maybe play a game of pin the tail on the master. After all, how many nights do they get to howl to their hearts' content?

THE MENU

Cucumber Salad (page 45)

Steak and Kidney Pie (page 92)

Sausage Cheese Grits (page 21)

Sautéed Collard Greens with Bacon and Corn Bread (page 44)

Coco Loco Bites (page 112)

Party Pup Cakes with Apple and Cheddar (page 105)

A Canine Cotillion

You want to do the right thing. Your heart is in the right place. Why not throw an outdoor dance in the summer for all your dog-loving friends? Make it a charity event to benefit your local animal shelter. In fact, if you've got a good relationship with your shelter, you might even ask them to set up a booth with dogs for adoption.

This could become an annual event for your community. Think big. Send out notices by e-mail, put one in the local newspaper, let your local TV and radio stations know about it.

To keep yourself from becoming totally crazed, make this a potluck supper. Ask every person to bring a dog (dressed in his finest dancing duds, of course), a covered dish, and a contribution to the local animal shelter. Give out dog prizes: Best Dressed, Best Behaved, Best Beast. You get the idea.

Choose your favorite recipe from this book, make a double or triple order, and let your friends bring what they will.

APPENDIX A

Foods to **NEVER** Feed Your Dog

To learn more about how to take care of your dog, check out *www.aspca.org*, click on Pet Care, and then click on Make Your Pet's Home Poison Safe.

The ASPCA lists the following foods as dangers to dogs:

- Alcoholic beverages (The small amounts of alcohol that are found in a few of our recipes will cook off and won't harm your dog.)
- Avocado
- Chocolate (in any form)
- Coffee (in any form)
- Fatty foods (The meats used in these recipes are generally quite lean.)
- Macadamia nuts
- Moldy or spoiled foods (This includes the bottom half of the 40-pound dried kibble bag, which is almost always rancid and may also be moldy.)
- Onions, onion powder, scallions, or shallots
- Products sweetened with xylitol
- Poultry or pork bones
- Raisins and grapes
- Tomato leaves, unripened fruit
- Yeast dough

The list of potentially hazardous items found around the house goes on:

- Antifreeze
- Cleaning chemicals
- Dental floss
- Electrical cords
- Fluoride toothpaste
- Garden chemicals
- Nutritional supplements
- Ointments containing vitamin D
- Poisonous toads
- Prescription drugs (for humans and dogs)
- Rat poison
- Rubber bands
- Rubber gloves
- Sticks
- String
- Tennis balls
- Wild mushrooms

Any of these and a hundred other things around the house can send a pup to the hospital.

APPENDIX B

Commercial Dog Foods You Should Look For (When You Need Them)

We know it isn't always possible to feed your dog home-cooked foods. And we do rely on certain dry kibbles and, on occasion, canned foods.

We believe that variety is the spice of life. Don't choose one brand of dog food and feed it day in and day out until hell freezes over. Would you like that kind of diet? We think not, but there are other reasons as well. The quickest route to developing food allergies is to eat one kind of food over and over again.

To find out where these products are sold, call or check the manufacturer's Web site. Some sell direct, and others offer their products through select pet food retailers.

Recommended Dry Dog Foods

- Solid Gold Dog Formula: *www.solidgoldhealth.com*
- Pet Promise: (800) 416-4700, *www.petpromiseinc.com*
- Bil-Jac: *www.biljac.com*
- Chicken Soup for the Dog, Diamond Pet Food
- Artemis "Natural 6 Mix": (800) 282-5876, *www.artemispetfood.com*

- Bench & Field "Holistic National Canine Formula":
  (800) 525-4802, available at Trader Joe's
- Burns "Brown Rice & Ocean Fish":
  (877) 983-9651, *www.burnspethealth.com*
- Drs. Foster & Smith "Adult Maintenance Formula, Chicken
  & Brown Rice": (800) 826-7206, *www.drsfostersmith.com*
- Go! Natural "Super Premium Chicken, Fruit & Vegetable
  Diet": (866) 864-6112, *www.forpaws.ca*
- Royal Canin "Natural Blend Adult Formula":
  (800) 592-6687, *www.royalcanin.com*
- Prairie Lamb Meal and Oatmeal: (888) 519-7387,
  www.naturesvariety.com
- VeRUS "GP Advantage Diet: Chicken Meat, Oats & Brown
  Rice": (888) 828-3787, *www.veruspetfoods.com*

Recommended Canned Dog Foods

- Artemis "Best Formula":
  (800) 282-5876, *www.artemispetfood.com*
- Drs. Foster & Smith "Lamb and Brown Rice":
  (800) 826-7206, *www.drsfostersmith.com*
- Newman's Own Organics "Organic Chicken":
  www.newmansownorganics.com
- Prairie "Duck": (888) 519-7387, *www.naturesvariety.com*
- Spot's "Stew": (800) 364-4256, *www.halopets.com*

Books to Put into Your Well-Dog Library

The Complete Herbal Handbook for the Dog and Cat, Juliette de Baïracli Levy, Faber and Faber, 1955.

The basis for all our study of small animal health. If you can read only one book, let this be it.

Dr. Pitcairn's Complete Guide to Natural Health for Dogs & Cats, Richard H. Pitcairn, D.V.M., Ph.D. and Susan Hubble Pitcairn, Rodale Press, 1995.

Everything you need to know to home-doctor your dog. From puppies to grief therapy after your best friend is gone, Dr. Pitcairn covers it.

Veterinarian's Guide to Natural Remedies for Dogs, Martin Zucker, Three Rivers Press, 1999.

This easy-to-use handbook includes recommendations from a number of holistic vets covering subjects from diet to disease with holistic remedies and explanations made simple.

Raw Dog Food: Make It Easy for You and Your Dog: Carina Beth MacDonald, Dogwise Publishing, 2003.

Want to know more about going whole hog into a raw diet for your dog? This book has the answers. Feed a whole chicken to a dog? Wonder what to serve as a side? This book takes you there.

Food Pets Die For: Shocking Facts about Pet Food, Ann N. Martin, foreword by Dr. Michael W. Fox, New Sage Press, 1997.

Everything you never wanted to know about commercial dog food.

Index